What others are saying about this book:

"It's comprehensive and informative, but best of all, it's extremely accessible to current/future teachers whose blood usually runs cold at the mention of 'linguistics' or 'grammar.' The conversational style and humorous tone are tremendously effective. . . ."

Dr. Peter Lowenberg, Associate Professor
Dept. of Linguistics and Language Development
San Jose State University, CA

"Dr. West has distilled the critical components of linguistics and described them with fine metaphors and good humor!"

Dr. Lois Locci, former Director of Education
University of California Santa Cruz Extension

"Steve West has done an amazing job of taking the mystery out of linguistics for teachers. This is a 'must have' resource for any teacher working with English learners. Dr. West writes with clarity, precision, and humor!"

Dr. Connie Casagranda Williams
Specialist in Second Language Acquisition

"The book is very compact but also very clear and instructive. It follows a perfectly arranged path which increases comprehension while its style simplifies a hard-to-understand academic area. It certainly is a reference book every English teacher would need. I wish I had had it when I was taking the course the first year at Berkeley."

Hayriye Karliova, MA, ESL Instructor
Marmara University, Istanbul, Turkey

D0926147

Linguistics for Educators
A Practical Guide

Second Edition

With Exercises

Steven Landon West, Ph.D.

International Institute of Language and Culture (IILC)
Richmond, California

Linguistics for Educators
A Practical Guide

Second Edition

by Steven Landon West, Ph.D.

Published by:
International Institute of Language and Culture (IILC)
3712 Stoneglen North
Richmond, CA 94806
USA

Orders: www.linguisticsforeducators.com

ISBN:
2nd edition: 978-0-9778-0291-3
Answer Key: 978-0-9778-0292-0

Printed in the United States of America

Table of Contents

Exercises

Dedication to

Rosie

My partner in love, in fun and in co-creation.

I couldn't have done it without you!

Acknowledgements

The creation of *Linguistics for Educators* was prompted by the thousands of students I have taught over the past ten years in these courses: *Fundamentals of Linguistics, Second Language Acquisition, Grammar for ESL Teachers* and *Cross-Cultural Communication.* Many of them are teachers who are looking for ways to broaden their own education for expansion into ESL teaching.

Of all the courses I give, linguistics is the one that provokes the most apprehension. However, the students' eagerness to deepen their understanding of our native tongue in spite of their fears has been the inspiration for the creation of this book. Their responsiveness has pointed me toward that middle ground between the best that linguistics has to offer and what is actually useful in the classroom. Many thanks to those forward-looking students/teachers.

Also, this book would not have come to fruition without the encouragement of Dr. Connie Casagranda Williams, a specialist in Second Language Instruction. In her awareness of what is meaningful to students in the classroom, she has guided me directly into that middle ground described above. Many, many thanks.

Special recognition belongs to V. Fromkin, R. Rodman and N. Hyams for their wonderful book, *An Introduction to Language* (now in its 8th edition). I continue to use it as a foundation for courses in linguistics. This book and Steven Pinker's *The Language Instinct* (a national bestseller) are wonderful combinations of thoroughness and unstoppable humor. They are "must reads" for anyone who is serious about the teaching of any language.

Chapter 1

Linguistics – Why Bother?

The purpose of this book is to provide you with information about the building blocks of English that is easily understood and practical to use. With the structural framework provided here, you will become a better guide for all your students in whatever field you teach. You will come to understand why your students make mistakes in English and how you can help them make the necessary corrections because finally they will be able to see clearly what the structures of correct sentences actually are.

There is not a teacher on earth who is not using, manipulating and teaching linguistics all day long at school, no matter what the subject. It is impossible to avoid it. Even if you are a PE teacher, a math teacher, an art teacher, a teacher of autistic children or a deaf teacher teaching deaf students entirely in a sign language, you are using linguistic structure throughout your lessons.

Many who use this book are native speakers of English, and many others have learned English as a second or foreign language. We will explore the miracle that is language by uncovering exactly what it is that we know when we know a language. Most of us know the basic features of linguistics; we can't help it. Anyone who has control of any human language knows these features almost intuitively.

It is just that we don't know exactly what it is that we know. In this book you will learn how to objectify your knowledge (learning how to name what you know) so that you can then deliver more effective instruction to your students.

You will learn the relevant concepts, skills and strategies at the core of language science in a way which makes them understandable and useful for people who are not specialists in linguistics.

For example, if you are a native speaker of English, you may never have thought much about how you make the sound at the beginning of the word *pill*. This is spelled [p] in the **International Phonetic Alphabet** (no surprise there; just wait for others that are not so clear). It's called a *voiceless bilabial stop.* We need not waste too much time with this fancy name, but when teaching someone who does not have this sound in their mother tongue, it certainly is practical and useful to be able to say to your learner: "First, don't 'buzz' your vocal chords; just let the air come through your mouth quietly, as if you were whispering. Second, close your mouth and keep it closed while you build up a moderate quantity of pressure behind your two closed lips (PSI, just like the pressure in the tires of your car). Then, still not buzzing your vocal chords, release your lips and produce a small explosion. That will make the sound. Practice it in isolation from the rest of the word. Don't say the name of the letter; just say its sound[1]: 'p-p-p-p.' Notice that it has a twin: [b]. These are not identical twins; rather, they are fraternal twins, the voicing being the only difference."

If your students are native speakers of Spanish, you, as their teacher, need to be aware that there is a major difference between the English pronunciation of this sound and the Spanish one. Speakers of English tend to "aspirate" [p] such that a noticeable puff of air follows the release of this sound, while speakers of Spanish do not aspirate this sound at all. Speakers of both languages need to discover just what these differences are and what causes them.

If your students are native speakers of Arabic, this exercise is very practical from a different point of view since Arabic does not have a *voiceless bilabial stop.* It only has its twin, a *voiced bilabial stop*: [b].

> **Phoneme** (preliminary definition): A distinctive sound of a given language. Standard American English has 40 phonemes.

Native speakers of Arabic don't have a need to even know about the [p] sound because they never use it in Arabic. Until they become aware of the distinction, many Arabs will tend to pronounce *people* as "beeble" [bibəl][2]. They don't even "hear" the sound of the [p]. What this means is that [p] is not a **phoneme** in Arabic (don't worry about this concept now; we will explore it later). Since it looks as though the action is between the lips, without your understanding of linguistics, you might find that you, as the teacher, and your Arabic speaking students will focus on the front of the mouth. The distinction has nothing at all to do with this part of the mouth, and this approach will only make the problem worse. It is entirely in the vibrating or the lack thereof of the vocal chords, completely at the other end of the speech making apparatus.

---

[1] Get into the habit of producing only the physical result of a distinct sound in English and not saying its name. Its name is usually misleading. For example, the name for [p] in English includes voicing. That is in the last part of its "name," but the sound itself has no voicing at all.

[2] This is the way of writing the sounds of this word in the International Phonetic Alphabet (please see the inside of the back cover).

You will soon discover precisely what we are doing when we make such sounds in English. You will then learn how to give your students practical suggestions about how to really improve[3] pronunciation, the biggest and potentially the most humiliating challenge for learners of English.

Test Your Knowledge (Exercise 1)
"Using the IPA"

Become familiar with the sounds of English and their "real" spellings in the IPA
(International Phonetic Alphabet – See the inside back cover):

<u>In written English</u>   <u>In the IPA (Don't bother with caps)</u>

1. Your first name: _____   _____

2. Your last name: _____   _____

3. Your home town: _____   _____

4. Your state: _____   _____

5. Your country: _____   _____

Learning a New Language: A "Minefield"

Many of us who are native speakers of English have had a less-than-sterling experience trying to learn a foreign language. I often hear comments from my students such as, "I hate (name of language). The teacher was arrogant, didn't really help us, and, furthermore, why the heck did we have to 'conjugate' verbs? All we did in class was talk about the language, translate and do boring grammar drills. The teacher made us feel so stupid because we could not get it. That is the first time in my life that I flunked a course, and I will never study a foreign language again."

---

[3] How could a "split infinitive" creep into a text such as this? The "Bishop" would roll over in his grave. In 1762 Bishop Robert Lowth wrote a book (*Short Introduction to English Grammar*) that has had impact far beyond its value even up to the present day. He and other English grammarians of the time made the subjective decision that infinitives should never be split, but as anyone observing modern written American English can see, infinitives are being split all over the place, even in distinguished works of literature.

Anyone who wants to gain fluency or control of a foreign language will go through a minefield to get there. Our job, as effective teachers of English, is to help ELs "defuse these mines" and get through unscathed. The learners mentioned above got blown up so many times that they decided to avoid the humiliation and never study the language again. Why do you think that most of us Americans are monolingual?

In order to help learners traverse the minefield, we first have to know just what each mine looks like from the learner's point of view. Our own knowledge of English is no help here. For example, the only way to see what that "mine" looks like from the point of view of a speaker of Zulu[4] is for us teachers to begin to understand some of the grammatical features of Bantu languages, the language branch to which Zulu belongs. The fact that you have an interest in Zulu and are willing to learn some of its features gives a powerful cultural/linguistic message of inclusiveness. That inclusiveness can be transformed into an effective "mine sweeper" for the learner.

Linguistics:"Almost a Science"

We might call linguistics a "soft science." It is as scientific as you can get in analyzing a phenomenon that is intensely human and subjective. It places a scientific framework onto an entity that never sits still. It is like trying to ride a tiger. When you teach this language, you are trying to keep the tiger on the road, but that is next to impossible to do. In addition, you are the one to whom students look for answers. You are the authority; so, you must continue to hold onto the reins even when it might feel as though you are about to be bounced into grammatical chaos.

> **Linguistics:** The study of the structure of a language, almost a science. This is a very broad discipline, including phonology, morphology, semantics and syntax.
> **Grammar:** The study of the rules and patterns of the "correct" forms of a given language. It focuses primarily on the morphology and syntax of a language.

You will find that it is helpful to be neither too **descriptive** (simply describing the language as it is without judgment, and, therefore, just letting the language flow along without guidance) nor too **prescriptive** ("prescribing," that is, prejudging what the language should be and insisting that there is only one proper way to speak or write English). Perhaps you have had a very prescriptive English teacher in your past who used moralistic anger to insist on "proper English." There is no

---

[4] Zulu is an example of a click language. Clicks are implosive sounds made by bringing air into the mouth rather than blowing air out (all of the sounds of English are made by blowing air out). Zulu borrowed this phonological feature from the Khoisan language family. All of these languages are spoken in southern Africa.

such thing as fixed, proper English if for no other reason than that during the time you read this paragraph the language has already moved on to something new. You will need to make a choice in the spectrum between **prescriptive** and **descriptive grammar** in your teaching. Both approaches have something to offer:

Where are you as a teacher on this spectrum?

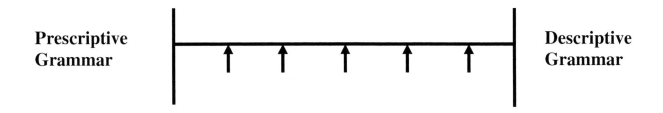

Prescriptive Grammar

Descriptive Grammar

Examples:
1. Never allow your students to end sentences with prepositions.
2. Always require your students to use "whom" in sentences such as "To whom are your speaking?"
3. Never allow "split infinitives" such as "to totally agree."

Examples:
1. Allow your students to use words like *wanna, gonna, Duh,* etc. even in writing.
2. Provide no corrections to students' written assignments even when grammar mistakes are obvious.

Add your own examples:

Add your own examples:

Test Your Knowledge (Exercise 2)
"Prescriptivism vs. Descriptivism"

Become aware of your own choices on the spectrum presented above.
How prescriptive or descriptive are you as a teacher?

1. Do you allow your students to <u>write</u> in the following ways:
"Who are you talking to?"
"I want you to really learn these verbs."
"She is bigger than me."
"Me and him are going to the game tonight?"
Words such as: "gonna, wanna, gotta, Duh"

      If yes, why?
      If no, why not?

2. Do you maintain a different standard for writing than for speaking?

3. How do you justify this double standard?

4. How will you manage this "can of worms" that you have opened for your students?

5. Are you encouraging your students to become more prescriptive or more descriptive?

6. What is your plan for making this happen?

A Brief History of English

It is helpful to remember that, from a strictly linguistic point of view, a language lasts about a thousand years, and during that period it goes through relentless changes. No one can stop those changes, no matter how hard one tries. If we had the bard of the poem *Beowulf* in our classroom today reciting this poem from the 8th century, we would not understand a word of the recitation. Looking at it in written form, we can begin to see resemblances to words we know in English (this is "Old English"). If Geoffrey Chaucer were with us reciting his *Canterbury Tales* of more than 600 years ago

(Middle English), we would undoubtedly understand much of it, but it is safe to predict that we would be in for some serious surprises as to the pronunciation of his language. This would also be true if we heard William Shakespeare reciting his own plays, though his works belong to the beginning of Modern English. And, by the way, what about those 2,000+ new words which Shakespeare coined in his plays? Do you suppose that his parents or his teachers would have approved of such an unorthodox, "descriptive" approach to "The Proper English" of the time? He jolted this language into new territory with the power of his pen.

As if this weren't difficult enough, you probably have noticed that there is a massive rift between written and spoken English. It is, indeed, a serious problem for any learner. Essentially what we write in the new millennium belongs to the English of the 1400s. When William Caxton introduced the printing press in 1475, he did his best to chart a middle and moderating course among the linguistic forces he faced such as regional variations and "ancient terms" that made English sound more like Dutch. English was, indeed, much closer to Dutch in his day than it is now. The following is from a story he presented in the introduction to his translation of a French work into English. In the story a man was requesting eggs from a "goode wyf," but she misunderstood him when he said he wanted "egges." Only when another person pointed out to her that he was talking of "eyren" did she understand. Caxton continues:

> Loo, what sholde a man in thyse dayes now wryte, egges or eyren? Certaynly it is harde to playse every man by cause of dyversite & change of langage. For in these days every man that is in ony reputacyon in his countre, wyll utter his commynycacyon and maters in suche maners & termes that fewe men shall understonde theym. And som honest and grete clerkes have ben wyth me, and desired me to write the moste curyous terms that I coude fynde. And thus bytwene playn, rude, & curyous, I stande abashed. But in my judgemente the comyn terms that be dayli used ben lighter to be understonde than the olde and auncyent englysshe. And for as moche as this present booke is not for a rude uplondyssh man to laboure therin, ne rede it, but onely for a clerke & a noble gentylman that feleth and understondeth in faytes of armes, in love & in noble chyvalyrye, therfor in a meane bytwene bothe I have reduced & translated this sayd booke in to our englysshe, not ouer rude ne curyous, but in suche termes as shall be understanden, by goddys grace, accordynge to my copye (quoted from McCrum 1986:86).

Notice that this does not look much like Modern English writing. Even though writing is linguistically much more conservative (resistant to change) than speaking, still the writing has changed dramatically in the past 600 years. Nevertheless, is it useful to note just how many words are close to their Modern English spelling with, perhaps, a letter or two different.

Nearly 600 years separate us from the language to which much of our spelling belongs. Now, when we write "Modern English" we are essentially writing Middle English. It creates tremendous difficulty for natives as well as for ESL students. We have found that there is only one spelling rule that is consistent: "Develop a personal relationship with every word you learn."

A teacher of English needs to acquire a basic understanding of where English comes from. This understanding provides the real reasons why English is the way it is and why words are written as they are in the modern day. If a student asks you, "Why is there a *w* in *answer?*" the reason for this can be found only in the history of the language. It may or may not be useful for the specific students you are teaching to delve into the history of English words (**etymology**), but one excellent way for you to prepare for your class is to examine this to a degree. It gives you that all important "backdrop" to your teaching, but be careful; you might find it to be fascinating.

English belongs to the Germanic branch of the Indo-European language family. Its Anglo-Saxon roots tie it deeply to the other Germanic languages in a grammatical sense. So, why are there so many French words in English? Considerably more than half of the vocabulary of English is French or Latin through French. The Norman version of French had a profound influence on English from the 11th to the 14th centuries. English was flooded with the French terms for nearly all of the social institutions that the Normans introduced. Despite this flood of words, the "glue" that held an English sentence together always remained and continues to remain Anglo-Saxon. Essentially, the French words that came into English were **content words**. These are nouns, verbs, adverbs and adjectives. They are full of meaning but relatively lacking in grammatical power. French had little influence on the **function words** of English. These are the prepositions, pronouns, conjunctions, articles, auxiliary verbs, etc. It is often difficult to define them precisely, but they are very powerful grammatically. They are the primary "glue" which holds a sentence together.

> **Content words:** the "open class" of words (nouns, verbs, adjectives & adverbs) which are filled with meaning and carry a limited amount of grammar in a sentence. They are quite flexible and have a "sense of humor."
> **Function words:** the "closed class" of words which are limited in meaning but carry powerful grammatical force (pronouns, prepositions, conjunctions, articles & auxiliary verbs). Unlike content words, function words are rigid; they have no sense of humor.

Test Your Knowledge (Exercise 3)
"Content words vs. function words"

1. What does it mean when we say that content words are "full of meaning but relatively lacking in grammatical power?" Create your answer in your own words:

2. What is "open" about content words?

3. What does it mean when we say that function words are limited in meaning but "carry powerful grammatical force."

4. In what way are they "closed?"

5. Make up a new word that has never been spoken before and determine whether it is a content word or a function word:

6. Create a verb phrase consisting of at least 3 words. In this VP, which are the content words and which are the function words? Can function-word auxiliary verbs sometimes become content words?

English has an amazing and very complicated history, and all of it comes to play in our modern version of it. In order for any of us to get command of it, we have no choice but to move forward through the modern results of its heavy history. We must incorporate medieval patterns, linguistic concepts and habits of spelling belonging to the early years of the last millennium, just to gain control of the language today.

What if we were to abandon the writing system of Modern English (really Middle English) and carry out a reform so that we would "get what we see" when we read English? What if spoken English were as close to its writing as spoken Spanish is to the writing of it? At first glance, this sounds tempting. We would no longer need spelling bees, and the need for the ridiculous amount of time and effort we put into the spelling of English would evaporate.

George Bernard Shaw vehemently suggested that we should carry out such a drastic language reform, advocating a new writing system in which the spoken language would accurately be reflected in the writing. While one can see the benefit of this, we would be cut off from such wonderful writing as Caxton's and those incomparable works of Geoffrey Chaucer, not to mention the works of William Shakespeare and even the *Gettysburg Address* of Abraham Lincoln. We would become alienated from them.

Such language reform would result in the following for the beginning of Lincoln's incomparable three-minute speech, prepared by hand on a sheet or two of paper and billed simply as "Dedicatory Remarks" (Wills 1992:34-35) on November 19, 1863:

> For skor ən sɛvən yərz əgo aur faðərz brɔt forθ ɔn ðɪs kantɪnənt, ə nu nešən, kənsivd ɪn lɪbərti, æn dɛdɪketəd tu ðə prapəzɪšən ðæt ɔl mɛn ar krietəd ikwəl.[5]

It is more comforting and less alienating, as part of our cultural history, to see the speech in the wonderful inconsistency of standard written English:

> ***Four score and seven years ago our fathers brought forth on this continent, a new nation, conceived in liberty, and dedicated to the proposition that all men are created equal.***

Need for Patience

One of our biggest challenges in becoming effective ESL teachers is the fact that we natives never did **learn** English; we **acquired** it. Our knowledge of English went into our brains as children on such a deep level, in such an unconscious way, that it is really difficult for us to articulate much of what we know about English. So much of it is just a "feeling." That is no help for an EL who does not have that feeling and must embark on an arduous journey of diligently studying and analyzing the idiosyncrasies of English.

---

[5] This is my own estimation in the IPA of the way he may have read it. No one can prove or disprove any part of this phonetic transcription, since we have no audio recordings of his actual speech.

A basic truth about education is that when it comes to teaching the knowledge that came to us as children, we can become amazingly impatient, especially with our adult students. That very impatience will shut down the EL's right brain (the enjoyable part of learning) so that we can become ineffective teachers.

Test Your Knowledge (Exercise 4)
"Check your patience as an ESL instructor"

Assuming that you are a native speaker of GAE (General American English),
consider some aspects of your linguistic knowledge about which you
might become impatient as an ESL instructor:

1. What are some aspects of the pronunciation of the sounds of American English that perhaps you have never thought of before and which could create real challenges for ELs? English is an intonational language, and this has a powerful influence on the organization of sounds within words and throughout sentences.

2. Have you ever thought about how you use those 3 little words: *a, an,* and *the*? Do you have the feeling that everyone should just know them because they are so simple? Many grammarians believe that the articles are unteachable to people who have not acquired English as their mother tongue. Why might this be true?

3. Why can we speakers of English say:
> "We pruned the trees in the afternoon." (or)
> "In the afternoon we pruned the trees."

but neither:

> "We in the afternoon pruned the trees." (nor)
> "We pruned in the afternoon the trees."

Without becoming irritated, how will you explain all of this to an EL who sees no problem with all 4 sentences? Notice how quickly you recoil from the 3rd and 4th sentences and how difficult it is to explain why you did so. Give your best explanation, especially the reasons for your adamant attitude about this:

4. Other aspects of English about which you might become impatient:

So, we need to slow down when we teach patterns of English that are so "obvious" to everyone. They are not at all obvious to ELs outside of the **linguistic fortress** of native fluency in English. For many learners fluency in English does, indeed, seem to lie beyond an impenetrable wall. We need to understand what the EL brings to the learning process. It is a similar story to what we natives bring to the process of trying to learn a foreign language. Patterns in English are so different, so alien to everything an EL has learned throughout her/his life, that incorporating this or that English pattern is extremely difficult.

For example, Chinese, Russian, Japanese, Turkish, Korean and many other languages do not have articles[6] (those three little words: *a, an* and *the*). It is easy for native speakers of English to ignore this issue; after all, they are simply three tiny words, and everybody understands them, right? And if they don't, what's their problem? These three little words can create life-long challenges to people from these languages even though they may have had many years of English study throughout their education. And, when you correct their writing in which these articles are misused over and over, you will likely have a hard time telling your students exactly why you inserted a *the* in a particular part of the text and removed it in another part. You will be relying on a "feeling" about its correct use. You will likely be correct, but you will have a hard time giving useful information to your student as to why you made those choices.

Need for Practical Linguistics

It is time for all of us to lighten up about language and grammar. If we can remove moralistic attitudes concerning the teaching of grammar and can begin to incorporate the essential and relevant features of linguistics into our instruction, we will then be able to find a way out of our own illiteracy and give all of our ELs effective and efficient stepping stones leading to control of English.

In terms of mastery of General American English, we have a national crisis on our hands. In 1992[7] the National Institute for Literacy (www.nifl.gov) prepared a survey in which it identified five levels of literacy:

---

[6] Many linguists put articles into a new class of words called **determiners.** However, this is not a useful concept for the purposes of this course. Also, see footnote #1 on p. 39.
[7] The results tabulated for 2005 show little change from this pattern.

➢ People at Level 1 (21 to 23% of adults) "can read a little but not well enough to fill out an application, read a food label, or read a simple story to a child."

➢ People at Level 2 (25 to 28% of adults) "can perform more complex tasks such as comparing, contrasting, or integrating pieces of information," but they do not have skills of "higher level reading and problem-solving."

➢ People at Levels 3, 4 and 5 have successful levels of literacy.

➢ People at Levels 1 and 2 (more than half of the adult population if viewed at the highest percentages shown above) "lack a sufficient foundation of basic skills to function successfully in our society."

The results of this survey show us that nearly one fourth of adult Americans are functionally illiterate, and nearly one half cannot function successfully because of their limited literacy skills.[8] Every year we turn out nearly a million new high school graduates in this nation who are functionally illiterate.[9] How could such a high degree of functional illiteracy take place?

There was something to be said for a more prescriptive approach to the learning of English in the 1950's and 60's. During that period the Reed and Kellogg sentence diagrams were still being used in English classes in the USA. Those of us who used them at that time regard them with nostalgia. They were a wonderful beginning, but they became obsolete because they were unable to show the all-important hierarchy of the constituents of a sentence. So, not only the diagrams, but the whole approach of analyzing the language essentially disappeared from the curriculum. By the 1980's "Whole Language" became the rage, and scientific viewing of the language essentially disappeared from the landscape. As a result, many teachers who were students during those years have very little awareness of concepts such as the parts of speech, tense and aspect for verbs, relative clauses, etc.

If the structure of English has, therefore, disappeared from the minds of many educated Americans, what should we do now? Teachers must acquire basic knowledge of the **nuts and bolts of language**. That is the purpose of this book.

---

[8] It should be noted that essentially no one in the USA is truly illiterate. Many more people than ever before are writing English on the keyboards of their electronic devices. Thus, the quantity of writing may have increased, but the quality of the grammar is often of a very dubious nature.

[9] Out of an approximate total of 2,800,000 annual high school graduates for the early 1990s, 25% (700,000) were unable to read their own diplomas (*Statistical Abstract of the United States:*1990 & 2002:tables 251 & 200 respectively).

Preview of Coming Attractions

In Chapter 2, the study of **morphology,** we will learn about **morphemes** as either complete words or parts of words. They have full or partial meaning, and they cannot be further reduced. For example, *book* is a morpheme, and *-s* is another morpheme. *Book* can stand alone as a **free morpheme** or a word, but *–s* must be attached to a word in order to have a life in English (i.e., a **bound morpheme**). *Books* is a word consisting of two morphemes. An understanding of the function of morphemes can help a learner to create a chain reaction of vocabulary building.

Chapter 3 (**syntax**) takes us into the grammatical forces that hold a phrase or a sentence together. **Tree diagrams** give us an unprecedented and graphic visualization of the relationship between the **constituents** of a sentence and the grammatical hierarchies governing those constituents. Tree diagrams can be started as early as 3rd Grade. Children love them because they bring visual clarity to the sentence structures they already have in their brains.

In Chapter 4 (**semantics**) we will find **idioms,** **metaphors** and the **–nyms** (synonyms, antonyms, metonyms, retronyms, hypernyms, hyponyms, homonyms, etc.), all powerful tools to introduce students to the world of meaning.

> (Preliminary definitions)
> **Morphemes:** words or parts of words
> **Idioms:** expressions in which the words do not function in their normal ways.
> **Metaphors:** words for concepts that have jumped out of their normal semantic groupings to create special effects.
> **The –nyms:** groupings of words which belong together for specific semantic purposes.
> **Syntax:** the "glue" that holds sentences together.
> **Constituents:** all of the grammatical elements of a sentence.

Chapters 5 and 6 cover **Phonology,** the study of the sound system of a language. Chapter 5 presents perhaps the most fundamental concept in any language: **phonemes**. It is not enough just to able to define the term, though we have to begin with this. What is crucial is to see how we native speakers of English **perceive** these distinctive sounds of the language and exactly what we do in the preparation of the **phonetic realization** (Chapter 6) of these phonemes. It involves the process of **objectifying** the **highly subjective nature** of our linguistic knowledge of our mother tongue.

What follows is a pictorial summary of the linguistic journey you are about to take with Nim Chimpsky as your guide. The real Nim was a chimpanzee who was taught sign language in the 1970s to see if he had the capacity to learn human language.[10] The results of the research demonstrated that Nim was not able to learn much. You, however, have the command of the English language as a foundation from which to discover what the structure of that knowledge really is. If you combine your knowledge of English with the active conceptualization of the tools and skills you will find in each chapter of this book (the "villages" through which Nim will guide you), you can become quickly skilled in the art of guiding your own students into control of English, and that will be quite an accomplishment!

---

[10] This research by H. D. Terrace and his associates is discussed in Fromkin (2003:386-388).

Nim Chimpsky's Treasure Hunt
for Linguistic Skills

Village of Morphology
(Chapter 2)
Content words and
   function words
Morphemes
Prefixes and suffixes
Derivational morphemes
Inflectional morphemes
Lexical gaps
"Bartability"

Village of Syntax
(Chapter 3)
Constituents (words and phrases
   acting as grammatical units)
Syntactic categories
Tree diagrams
Grammatical hierarchy
Transitive and intransitive verbs
Embedded sentences
Deep structure and   "The Wozy
   transformations   Briggles"

Village of Semantics
(Chapter 4)
Homographs, homonyms,
   synonyms, antonyms and
other   "-nyms"
The centrality of verbs
Metaphors ("Semantic
   earthquakes")
Idioms
Pragmatics
"Semantic pockets"

Village of Phonology
(Chapters 5 & 6)
Phonetics and the IPA
Consonants and vowels
Voiced and voiceless sounds
Where and how sounds are
made
   in the mouth
Diphthongs
Phonemes and allophones
Minimal pairs
"English Phonemic Chip"
Tone and intonation

Please dog-ear this text and spill coffee on it. Make this your own working document. And, please let us know if you have suggestions for making the explanations even clearer. The goal is to translate the powerful concepts and skills from linguistics into a usable form for teachers.

Chapter 2

Morphology:
The Inner World of Words

Words live in two worlds: an **inner world** (morphology) and an **outer world** (syntax). This chapter concerns a word's inner world. What are its constituents? How receptive or unreceptive are these constituents toward other possible constituents of a word? What are the general patterns of word formation? If students can begin to conceptualize the inner workings of this world, they will discover a chain reaction of efficient learning and vocabulary building. A teacher can become a powerful catalyst to help students learn how to build vocabulary on their own.

What does a word actually consist of? As Fromkin[1] points out on p. 69: "A particular string of sounds must be united with a meaning, and a meaning must be united with specific sounds" in order to become a word. What is a "particular string of sounds?" As we will discover in Chapter 5, this string consists of one or more **phonemes** strung together in one direction (we could not say *tack* [tæk][2] for *cat* [kæt] and still have the same meaning). In order to have a life, this string must be fused with a particular meaning. Clearly a tack is not the same thing as a cat. All speakers of English agree that only a specific meaning can be fused with the sounds of *cat* and a completely different one with *tack*.

The English speaker saying [kæt] and the English speaking listener go through two complementary processes almost at the same time: 1. the English speaker forms the idea of a cat in her head, chooses the phonemes and the order needed for this concept, commands the mouth to make this string of sounds and releases it to the air for the listener; 2. the listener uses his ears to start the process essentially in reverse. The

---

[1] This is *An Introduction to Language* (2003, 7th edition) by V. Fromkin, R. Rodman and N. Hyams. We strongly recommend that you acquire this book. It can serve as a valuable resource throughout your teaching career.
[2] This word is written in the author's version of the IPA (the International Phonetic Alphabet). Please see the inside back cover for the full alphabet and Chapter 6 for a full explanation of this.

same or similar image of a cat is implanted in the brain of the listener. He places this string of sounds at the appropriate "shelf in the stacks" of his mental library, his **lexicon**[3], and fully understands what the speaker is talking about - a cat. In this process both agree that this string of sounds is combined with a particular meaning, i.e., the cat. Now we have a word that is relatively independent, ready to interact with other words in a phrase or sentence. This is **syntax,** which we will discuss in the next chapter.

Morphemes

Morphemes are the word builders of language. They are, as Fromkin points out, "the minimal linguistic unit. . . the arbitrary union of a sound and a meaning that cannot be further analyzed" (Fromkin 2003:76). They may be complete words, or they may be parts of words. *Cat* is both a complete word and a single morpheme. From the point of view of English, it cannot be reduced further. If we add an *–s*, we now have *cats,* a new word made up of two morphemes: *cat* and *–s.* Clearly *–s* cannot be reduced any further. It is not a word. Does *–s* have meaning? Yes, but its meaning is dependent; it relies on its attachment to *cats* in order for its meaning to emerge. *Cat* is a **free morpheme**, and *–s* is a **bound morpheme**. *–s* belongs to a small number of **inflectional morphemes** (a total of eight) that are extremely powerful in the English language. Please see the discussion below.

> **Free morpheme:** These are words which occur without any prefixes or suffixes and which can stand independently within the language (*cat*).
> **Bound morpheme:** These are parts of words. They are all prefixes or suffixes in English (the *–s* of *cats*) along with a small number of roots which can have a life in English only when attached to prefixes (*-ceive* in *receive*), suffixes or other roots (*boysen-* in *boysenberry*).

Prescription consists of three morphemes:

pre-   A prefix has meaning only when it is combined with a following word. Therefore, it is a **bound morpheme.** It carries the general meaning of "happening before."

---

[3]This is the Greek word for dictionary (a Latin word), and it refers to the "dictionary in our heads." This is an example of how English has grown in leaps and bounds across many centuries, taking a word from one language for a particular purpose and a similar one from another language, giving it a slightly different meaning. The metaphor of "shelves in the stacks" of our lexical libraries adds another useful connotation in that the words in our lexicons are grouped into many categories with varying criteria, much the same way that books are organized in a library, and not strictly "A to Z."

script   This is a root word which in this usage carries "verb energy." In line with the vast majority of root words, it has a life of its own, usually in its usage as a noun. Almost all root words are **free morphemes.**

-ion   This is a suffix which also has meaning only when combined with a preceding morpheme. It turns the verb into a noun which describes the process or the result of the action in the verb. It is another **bound morpheme.**

There is a particular order in the way that morphemes make up words. We can say *prescribe*, but we cannot say **scription*.[4] In this case, the prefix must attach first to make a new verb, and then we can add *–ion* to turn the whole thing into a noun.

Test Your Knowledge (Exercise 5)		
"How many morphemes are there in each word?"		
Anaconda	Organizational	Googling
Rats	Disambiguate	Prioritization
Uneventfully	Debugged	Downloaded
Reworking	Autobiography	Metacognitive
Impossibility	Psychologically	Inimitably

How can the understanding of morphemes help teachers in their attempts to elevate the linguistic awareness of their students? Memorizing long lists of vocabulary is one way of learning new words, but a far more effective way of learning words is to gain **leverage** in the process. Science teachers often wonder how linguistics can help them. Their field of study actually provides one of the clearest examples of acquiring leverage in learning vocabulary. If students can acquire an active understanding of the following morphemes and their combinations, they open the road to a chain reaction of vocabulary building. It is very important that students not just memorize the meaning of a final word; the key is for them to acquire an active understanding of the meaning of each prefix and suffix and apply that

---

[4] An asterisk will be inserted for words, phrases or sentences that are impossible in English.

understanding to any time in the future when those morphemes show up again in new words:

Prefix	Root word	Final word
milli-	*meter*	*millimeter*
centi-	*gram*	*centimeter*
kilo-		*meter*
		kilometer
		milligram
		centigram
		gram
		kilogram

Three prefixes and two root words (also morphemes) can generate leverage for a vocabulary list of eight words. The words *gram* and *meter* acquire new meaning because they are "placed" within a framework of larger and smaller units of measurement. Each time a student goes over such a list, the understanding of words and their morphemes deepens, and that is the key to gaining mastery of vocabulary.

Each time a teacher comes across words like *biology, geography, philosophy, synonym* or *metaphor,* he or she can see through these words and realize the potential of leveraging vocabulary by teaching the morphemes. Rather than stopping only long enough to learn one word in isolation, the teacher can make up games using the morphemes to build a **metacognitive** process in the minds of students so that they can begin to manage their own learning of vocabulary throughout their lives. They are putting **word power** into their **lexicons**. Think of a **metacognitive skill** as the development of one's internal **manager of the learning process.** Students can become their own teachers throughout their lives. Rather than responding passively to whatever a teacher delivers in the classroom, a student can assertively take control of the learning process. This is the key for success in college or in one's professional life, whatever the field.

Test Your Knowledge (Exercise 6)
"How many words can you make using the –*graph*- morpheme?"
(Give your students real word power!)

Content Words and Function Words

It is very helpful to think of language in broad categories. Often these are new categories which native speakers have never thought about before, but they know them well when they are pointed out. Such is the distinction between content words and function words. Think of content words as loaded with meaning and having a minimum of grammatical power. Think of function words as just the opposite: filled with grammatical power and a minimum of meaning.

There is a sense of freedom connected to **content words** (essentially nouns, verbs, adjectives and adverbs). On the one hand, they are very receptive. We can add new words to these four categories almost at will. Indeed, Silicon Valley never stops adding words to this **open class** of words, and new content words are coming into English from other languages at a dizzying rate. Not only that, we can play around with them and tamper with the sounds they stand for. Lewis Carroll and Dr. Seuss were relentless in their pursuit of **lexical gaps** (discussed below) to amuse us and to incite our imaginations.

Function words have no such humor. Think of prepositions, pronouns, articles and conjunctions. Though they are often hard to define, they have sticking power as they hold the sentence together for dear life, and since they are a **closed class,** they will not receive new words as members. Dr. Seuss and Lewis Carroll never tried to invent any new lexical gaps for the function words. We can see this process at work in the following famous lines from Carroll's "Jabberwocky," a ballad in his children's tale, *Through the Looking Glass:*

> 'Twas brillig, and the slithy toves
> Did gyre and gimble in the wabe.

He wouldn't dare tamper with *and, the, did* and *in.* In this case, *did* is considered an "auxiliary verb," not the main verb, and as such it is in the closed class. Depending on the context, *did* can be either a function word or a content word:

> *She did the job.* (content word)
> *She did understand the assignment.* (function word)

Free and Bound Morphemes

Many words of English consist of one morpheme. They can stand alone; their inner worlds are complete. They may belong to any of the parts of speech and need nothing more to interact grammatically with other words in the sentence: noun (*house*), verb (*go*), adjective (*bright*), adverb (*very*), pronoun (*she*), article (*the*), preposition (*in*), conjunction (*and*), interjection (*Wow!*) These are **free morphemes.** They can also be long words: *salamander, avocado, moccasin.*

Almost all **bound morphemes** in English appear in the form of two types of **affixes** (a general term to describe partial words added to other words to modify them): **prefixes** and **suffixes.** They are bound because they cannot stand alone. Their meaning emerges only once they are attached to a word: the prefixes *hypo-* and *hyper-* can be added to *sensitive* to give opposing meanings to this word. The suffixes *–ful* and

–less can be added to *help* to turn this noun into adjectives with very different meanings. A good dictionary will give separate entries for these prefixes and suffixes, showing that they are to be considered as important as individual words.

The combination of free and bound morphemes within words creates a chain reaction of vocabulary building. Students will profit tremendously by understanding this interplay. It is essential that, as early as possible, young students learn to know the common prefixes and suffixes of English, not just for the purpose of memorizing individual words to pass a spelling test, but to internalize the meaning of these affixes so that they can be applied hundreds of times throughout their lives as they encounter new words. When a teacher is building vocabulary with students, the time spent having them actively learn the general meanings of prefixes such as *pre-, pro-, re-, con-, a-, non-, un-, dis-* and suffixes such as *–able, -less, -ful, -ion, -ize* will go a long way toward helping students to gain leverage in their general education.

Single morpheme words such as *cat, give, house, school,* etc. can also be called **free roots**. They are content words and cannot be further reduced. They are self-sufficient and are prepared to receive any number of bound morphemes to enhance their meanings.

Morphemes such as *huckle-* and *–ceive* exhibit an unusual phenomenon in English. These, along with a relatively small number of other words, should be content words, but like bound morphemes, they do not have a life of their own in English. They are **bound roots** and must be attached to prefixes or suffixes in order to come alive in the language.

Derivational Morphemes

Bound morphemes are generally of two types: 1. those which primarily alter **meaning** in words (**derivational morphemes**), and 2. those which primarily alter **grammar** (**inflectional morphemes**). What exactly does this mean?

> **Derivational morphemes:** These are prefixes and suffixes which are added to words to change their syntactic categories, i.e., to change them to a different "part of speech." The verb *act* becomes the adjective *active* by the addition of *-ive*.
>
> **Inflectional morphemes:** These are exclusively suffixes which "hug" the word in question to give a different grammatical force. *Books* becomes pluralized by the suffix *–s*. *Worked* is put into the past tense by the addition of *–ed* to *work*.

Derivational morphemes change the syntactic categories (parts of speech), and, therefore, the meanings of thousands of words in English. For example, when we want to use the "meaning energy" of a verb for an adjective, English allows us to add a suffix to the verb to create a new word with a new meaning. Then, we can turn the adjective around to its opposite, and finally make the whole thing a new noun:

Morphemes	Results	New Meaning
accept (a verb)		
accept + able	acceptable	now an adjective
un + accept + able	unacceptable	another adjective with its opposite meaning, an **antonym**
un + accept + able + ty	unacceptability	a noun

This last example consists of four morphemes: one free morpheme (the verb) and three bound morphemes, two for adjectives and one for the noun.

Lexical Gaps

To show the flexibility in our understanding of words, we can tamper with the inner worlds of words to an amazing degree. When we read Lewis Carroll's two new verbs, *gyre* and *gimble*, in an unusual sort of way we "recognize" them. Somehow, they fit the English language.

How can this be? They never existed before Carroll created them. These are **lexical gaps**, and they fit two criteria: 1. They must be compatible with the sound requirements of English, and 2. They must be "available," that is, they have never been used as of yet. They are sitting there in the potential lexicon of English speakers waiting for some creative soul to bring them out.

Why can we almost recognize them? This is because they look and sound as though they could be words. They don't violate any of the sound requirements of English. If Carroll had written *gdimble,* for example, we would reject it and not make the effort to understand what he was writing, but since *gimble* sounds as though it could be a perfectly good word in English, we immediately set about trying to "fuse" some meaning onto the word, exactly the same process we apply to morphemes and words (a string of sounds fused with meaning). You will find that students will go to great lengths to try to explain exactly what *gimble* means, and the further they pursue this, the stronger they feel about its exact meaning.

It is good to create lexical gaps with students. It allows their linguistic imaginations to explore the formation of words outside a strict framework of vocabulary. That very exploration will give them a sense of freedom and objectivity to the words they know. They can watch the actual creation of new words in English:

glub	glube	gleeb	waglibby
slib	slube	sleeb	faslooby
glorn	florn	storn	kajorn
froozle	sloozle	joozle	kabloozle
kaphlam	gaslam	gafroozy	kazam
windooby	wyhooby	kaflooby	kadorn
dweely	dreely	fleezy	jakorn
hoopy	froopy	dwoopy	kabloom

"Bartability" and the Productivity of Morphemes

Recently the author asked an administrator in an office at UC Berkeley about a location in San Francisco. He had just moved to the Bay Area and was unfamiliar with downtown San Francisco but was having fun discovering the wonders of BART (Bay Area Rapid Transit). He asked her, "Is such and such address 'bartable?'"

It took her less than a second to say, "It is definitely 'bartable.'" He had never said the word nor heard it before, and the same is true for this woman. By the time this word was spoken, both he and she were, of course, familiar with the transformation of this acronym to a verb, *to bart*. It is from this verb that he created *bartable*, not from the noun it stems from.

I usually put this word on the board for my linguistics students and then watch them go on a morphological journey that boggles the mind:

BART	acronym, noun
to bart	verb
bartable	adjective, describing a place within walking distance of a BART station
bartability	another noun (One student told me that among her friends this means money. If she and a friend wanted to go somewhere on the BART system, she would say, "Do you have the bartability?")
to bartify	verb
bartification	noun (not enough of this yet in the Bay Area)
to debartify	verb
debartification	noun (a no-no for the Bay Area)
bartilicious	adjective, feeling transcendent while riding BART, possibly also munching on tasty snacks
bartifluous	adjective, flowing along happily on BART, rather oblivious to the surroundings
bartilosis	noun, abnormal use of BART
bartilitis	noun, the disease of using BART too much (Some people have been known to go to sleep on BART, going back and forth two or three times from the beginning to the end of a train line until 1:00 a.m. when BART shuts down. They have to pay as much as $75 for a taxi to get home.)

This is **rule productivity**. The bound, derivational morpheme, *-able* is one of the most powerful suffixes in the English language; it can start a chain reaction all by itself. We suggest that you do an exercise like this with your students. Pick a word and let them explore their own morphological creativity to reinforce their grasp of the structure of English.

Inflectional Morphemes

English used to be a highly inflected language. What exactly does this mean? Inflections are **affixes** that are attached to words to modify the grammar of that word in relation to other words in a sentence. All inflections for English involve nouns, pronouns, verbs and adjectives.

Declension refers to the inflection of nouns and adjectives, and **conjugation** refers to the inflection of verbs. We don't speak of these two concepts with much seriousness in English, and that is because there are so very few of these inflections left in the language. When we study other languages these two concepts give us headaches; we would rather not participate in them. However, if your mother tongue is filled with them, such as Spanish, Russian, German or Turkish, then these concepts resonate in your grammatical frame of mind, and the more we ESL teachers become aware of "where these speakers are coming from" in terms of their inflections, the better guides we can be for bringing them into the very different grammatical world of English.

As with many languages, Old English made use of "cases" (in the world of declensions) to express grammatical relationships primarily with nouns and pronouns. We still have vestiges of these cases today: The –'s of *Jill's book* is in the "genitive case." The *–m* in *For Whom the Bell Tolls* is another example. This case ending (used for dative and accusative cases) is disappearing from English. A majority of the thousands of English teachers who have taken my courses now consider *whom* to be obsolete. The removal of cases, and their resulting inflections, from English is a process of simplification that dates back to the use of Old English at a time when the British Isles were inhabited by speakers of many languages, and English was not yet the language of the land.

Researcher Tom Shippey has created a wonderful conversation in which a speaker of Old English is trying to sell his horse somewhere in England to a speaker of Old Norse. This scenario takes us back more than a thousand years:

Anglo-Saxon: "Ic selle the that hors the draegeth mine waegn."
(I'll sell you the horse that pulls my cart.)

"That hors" means one horse, but "tha hors" would mean two horses, and the Norseman probably would not be listening for this fine distinction since "hors" stays the same.

If the Norseman were to say this in his language, he would say, "Ek mun selja ther hrossit er dregr vagn mine."

At that time Old Norse and Old English were close enough to each other that each man speaking his own language would have been able to understand the other and be understood in a general sense, but because of the inflections in Old English, the Norseman could not be sure whether the Englishman is selling one or two horses. This detail is buried in the inflections, and the Norseman would not have been paying attention to such detail (McCrum 1986:70). For purely practical reasons, the inflections got in the way of communication, and eventually they almost disappeared from English.

The cases have disappeared one by one, across many centuries. In the present day we have just as much need to modify the grammatical approaches to nouns, pronouns, adjectives and verbs, but, in general, we put these words into a specific word order with no endings at all, or we employ prepositional phrases to serve these grammatical needs[5]:

> *I* (nominative) *will sell my* (genitive) *horse*
> (accusative) *to you* (dative) *for two pounds. It*
> (nominative) *is in a stable* (locative) *two miles*
> *from here* (ablative).

In this example, many other languages would put affixes (inflections) at the ends of the words in italics preceding the names of the cases and not worry so much about word order.

If you have only one or two cases in the form of inflections in a language such as English, or if you have only one verb form that regularly differentiates itself from all other forms (the 3rd person singular), then, there is really no point in talking about declension and conjugation at all. So, we don't, and, as a result, we speakers of English may be put off by the necessity to learn cases when we study other languages, such as German, Russian or Turkish. The value for ESL teachers is to realize that speakers of these languages are oriented toward the declension of nouns and adjectives as well as toward the conjugation of verbs. This is their framework for understanding much of their own grammar. We will become more effective teachers if we

---

[5] It is also important to note that, since we have no cases in English, word order takes on much more importance than it does for a language filled with cases. We will discuss this more in the chapter on syntax.

are aware of what declension and conjugation are and are able to show them that English serves these purposes essentially through the use of word order and prepositional phrases.

In many languages other than English, inflections typically are suffixes (they can also be other affixes) at the ends of nouns, pronouns, adjectives and other words that "hover" around nouns such as articles (now called **determiners**). They are used in many languages to show grammatical relationships within a sentence or a phrase.

The eight inflections we have left in English constitute the most powerful paradigm for teaching and learning English grammar within the inner world of words:

"English Inflectional Morphemes		Examples
-s	third-person singular present	She wait-**s** at home.
-ed	past tense	She wait-**ed** at home.
-ing	progressive	She is eat-**ing** the donut.
-en	past participle	Mary has eat-**en** the donuts.
-s	plural	She ate the donut-**s**.
-'s	possessive	Disa**'s** hair is short.
-er	comparative	Disa has short-**er** hair than Karin.
-est	superlative	Disa has the short-**est** hair."

(Fromkin 2003:101)

This list is so important that we recommend that ESL teachers keep it in mind throughout their teaching experience and bring it up at appropriate times. For example, if you are teaching the plural form of nouns, you will do well to remember that the other two mentioned in the above list are almost identical forms which the learner must be able to distinguish from each other. So, perhaps a follow-up lesson should briefly introduce those two other forms. Also, if you are working with a text for students which ignores any one of these eight forms, you know that you must introduce them so that these morphemes that have so much leverage in the language are not neglected.

38

Test Your Knowledge (Exercise 7)
"Derivational or inflectional morpheme?"

1. *Books*   5. *Booked*

2. *Impossible*   6. *Silliest*

3. *Seeing*   7. *Broken*

4. *Inactive*   8. *Exceedingly*

Test Your Knowledge (Exercise 8)
"The importance of morphemes"

1. What is the importance of understanding the morphemes added to the root words above?

2. Describe in your own words how your students' awareness of morphemes can create an explosion of vocabulary building for them:

Chapter 3

Syntax: The Glue of Phrases and Sentences

Syntax is what holds words together to produce a sentence. Here's how it works. First, a word's inner world must be completed by the combination of all relevant morphemes (*psyche* + *logos* = *psychology* +*-cal* = *psychological*). Then it is ready to enter its outer world, its contribution to the making of a sentence. This word sends out grammatical feelers to other words and phrases, letting them know that it will play one or another role in the assembling of a grammatically correct sentence. For example, *psychological* is an adjective, waiting to provide modification to a following noun: *psychological sense.* Adding the **article**[1] *a*, we

> **Syntax:** The grammatical cohesion that holds words and phrases together in a meaningful way and then allows them to become part of a well-ordered structure that produces a larger phrase or a sentence.

get *a psychological sense.* This grouping is called a **noun phrase.** The role this phrase plays in a sentence makes it a different kind of noun, and it is important for the learner to realize this. This grouping has a grammatical life of its own. The individual words and these groupings are called **constituents**, and it is essential that learners internalize this concept because it carries meaning from the smallest to the largest units of a sentence. When we add *in*, a **preposition**, we produce a **prepositional phrase**, yet another constituent in the sentence. *In a psychological sense* operates as a relatively independent constituent on a higher, more powerful grammatical level than any of the individual words in the phrase.

> **Constituent:** a unit of a sentence (typically a word, phrase or clause) that interacts grammatically and hierarchically in the formation of a sentence until the whole thing "jells" in the minds of competent speakers and competent listeners.

---

[1] The **articles** (*a, an,* and *the*) are an important part of what are now called **determiners.** We have avoided this last term because it is not consistent and is, therefore, confusing for an introduction to linguistics such as this book. For example, in *This is **my** book, my* is clearly a determiner (it determines the following noun). However, in *This book is **mine**,* this last word is not a determiner. It neither precedes nor determines anything following. It is a type of pronoun, and in the interest of consistency, it is better to leave these words as forms of pronouns. In the same way, the older term **article** preserves a better sense of consistency.

Before we take this phrase into the formation of a sentence, let's present its constituent parts and observe the grammar (syntax) at work:

Inner world of the word (its morphology):	*Psyche*	**Noun** (Greek)
	Logos	**Noun** (Greek)
	Psychology	**Noun** (English)
	Psychological	**Adjective** (English)
Outer world of the word (its syntax):	*Psychological*	**Adjective**
	A psychological sense	**Noun Phrase**
	In a psychological sense	**Prepositional Phrase**

We will present these concepts in more detail below as we move toward the formation of a sentence.

As you begin to put on your "syntactic antennae," you will sense the "glue" that binds the following sentences together or, perhaps, you will discover a lack of cohesion that makes us know instantly that the sentence is wrong. You may even recoil at the thought of such a word grouping being accepted as a grammatically correct sentence. Your very recoiling is proof of how well you know, internally, the grammar of English.

(a) *Suddenly Betsy gave him the ball.*

This sits comfortably in our minds with all of the constituents in order.

(b) *Suddenly Betsy gave him.*

We recoil immediately from this, knowing almost instinctively that something very important is missing. We know that *give* has peculiar characteristics. It is a **transitive verb** requiring that two objects follow it, a **direct object** (a noun phrase which can receive direct action from the verb) and an **indirect object** (the receiver of the thing being given). We want to come in and fix it, perhaps by saying, *Suddenly she gave it to him.*

(c) *Betsy gave him in the morning.*

Same problem. In the listener's mind he or she is screaming, "What did she give to him?" *Give* is a very fussy verb. The majority of the time it demands that the user provide two different objects. Notice that *suddenly* and *in the morning* are functioning in the same way in these sentences; they are both adverbs modifying *gave*. The entire prepositional phrase acts as an adverb.

(d) *Betsy gave him the package in the morning.*

Now we are happy. All constituents are in order, and the sentence sits there in royal comfort. Begin to notice how it is especially the verb that wants to find comfort and how it seems to order other constituents around to achieve that comfort.

(e) *Landon appeared the car.*

We recoil again. *Appear* is an **intransitive verb**; it does not want any of those direct objects following it. It is perfectly happy to live its life without putting any direct action on any following noun phrase.

(f) *Landon appeared next to the car.*

We are happy. *Appeared* wants to be left alone without objects but is both capable and willing to accept an adverb or two.

> **It is very important for students to acquire active conceptualization of this major division of verb types:**
>
> **Transitive verbs:** Verbs which apply direct action onto a following object: *hit, pull, grind, give, destroy.* In their main usage they require a direct object. They are simply "naked" in the sentence without them.
> **Intransitive verbs:** Verbs which, in their main usage, will not accept direct objects: *seem, appear, sleep, erupt, look, reply.*
>
> **This is a complicated story. All of the verbs listed under "transitive verbs" above can also serve intransitively. Students who hope to achieve command of English simply have to learn this.**

(g) *Logan considers Eric a jerk.*

Here again the verb is satisfied with the way the other words have lined up to fulfill its requirements. *Consider* is one of a small number of transitive verbs which take a direct object, which, in turn, takes an *object complement.* In this case, *Eric* is the direct object, and *a jerk* is the complement of that direct object, almost like saying, *Eric is a jerk.*

(h) *Logan considers a jerk.*

Something is wrong. Verbs are fussy, and will not tolerate having other words ignore their detailed requirements.

(i) *Logan considers me old-fashioned.*	This is also fine. In this case the *complement* to the direct object, *me,* is an adjective. The verb is appeased again.
(j) *Logan considers old fashioned.*	The verb simply will not stand for this. In order to be excellent teachers of English, we must bring our unconscious awareness of such grammatical requirements to the surface so that we can walk our ELs through these maddening details. The first thing that comes to mind in an EL's mind is the inconsistency of all of this.
(k) *Debbie put the curtains up with her neighbor.*	The verb is content again. What is *up* doing in this sentence? Is it a preposition? Describe the grammatical function of *with her neighbor.*
(l) *Debbie won't put up with her neighbor.*	What is going on here? Are *up* and *with* prepositions? Isn't this rather bizarre? What are these two "prepositions" doing here? What is really the verb of this sentence? What kind of a verb is it? Can you think of other verbs that could take the place of this phrasal verb? If an EL asks you why English has such odd expressions, what will you say? If someone asks a "why" question about the grammar of English and you can point to a strong grammatical principle that backs up the example, then you can answer the question. If the questioner wants to know why English is this way, there is no answer. It just is this way, and we natives and any learners of English can do nothing but accept it in all its wonderful inconsistency. These two sentences provide good examples of the importance of the **middle managers**[2] (in a grammatical sense) of a sentence. In (k) *with her neighbor* is clearly a prepositional phrase, but is it a prepositional phrase in (l)? To an EL, at first glance, it looks as though it should be. In reality, it has nothing to do with prepositional functions.

---

[2] These phrases are generally between whole sentences and words in terms of length. They are very important in that they govern and clarify the intermediate, hierarchical patterns of a sentence. In traditional grammars we have tended to ignore them, focusing primarily on the two extremes: words and sentences.

(m) *Humphrey did the project in the garage.*	A straightforward sentence. What kind of a verb is *did?*
(n) *Humphrey did in his friend in the garage.*	What is going on here? Can you come up with another verb to replace this phrasal verb? How would you name the infinitive of the verb? Just as in (l) above, the first *in* here is not a preposition at all. It is part of a **phrasal verb**, and it has a life of its own, totally unrelated to the function of prepositions. It is really an **idiom** (more on this later), in which the two words, *did* and *in,* are not being used in their normal way. They actually constitute a **transitive verb** which requires a direct object, *his friend,* and they are even so unorthodox as to be able to split up in the sentence and still retain their meaning.
(o) *Humphrey did it in the garage.*	How is *in* functioning in this sentence? Can you describe the role of the preposition and its phrase in this sentence?
(p) *Humphrey did the garage in.*	How can we take this "preposition" and put it at the end of the sentence? It looks like a "postposition" such as you will find in many languages such as Japanese or Turkish. Remember that people coming from languages such as these will have an instant grammatical response saying, "I recognize that grammar. That must be just like my mother tongue." They may not recognize that it has nothing at all to do with prepositional or postpositional phrases. The "outer world" of the morpheme *in* is completely different from its common usage. How can phrasal verbs be so unorthodox as to be able to split up in the sentence and still retain their meaning? There is no answer, and as an ESL teacher you will face many questions like this to which there is no answer. That is just the way English is.

(q) *In the garage* What have we done in this sentence? Looking ahead in
 Humphrey did it. the chapter we will see that this is a surface
         manifestation of a **transformation** from the original
         deep structure sentence and its surface manifestation,
         Humphrey did it in the garage.

Let's review our comprehension of syntax. Try to take the definition at the
beginning of the chapter and put it into your own words. As has been said before,
it is a crucial part of the knowledge we have about language in general and about
our own mother tongues in particular that **we know but don't know that we
know.**

The understanding of syntax is crucial because many of us native speakers of
American English along with our ESL students never achieved complete control of
this hierarchical structure. It got stunted somewhere along the way. It is our job,
as teachers, (1) to find, in the minds of our ELs, just where that stunting took place,
(2) to understand just what the structural misinformation consists of, and then (3)
to find ways to let the full grammatical structures come alive in their minds.

The word **syntax** is of Greek origin, and it means "to arrange together in order."
This is exactly what happens. Another definition of syntax is the arranging
together of the **constituents** of a sentence in a well-ordered hierarchy.

Understanding constituents is critical to grasping the overall function of syntax.
There aren't many linguistic terms which we need to add to the ones we learned in
English grammar courses in high school or in college, but this certainly is one of
them.

All of the following are constituents:

psychological	**Adjective**
sense	**Noun**
a	**Article**
a psychological sense	**Noun Phrase**
in	**Preposition**
in a psychological sense	**Prepositional Phrase** functioning as an **Adverb**

Syntax is the entire process of getting the constituents to jell. In effect, it provides
a test for each sentence created. As long as each sentence passes the "syntax test,"
the speaker or the writer may continue uninterrupted in a continuous flow of

discourse. This is a crucial part of **fluency.** However, even if only one constituent misfires (that is to say, does not fulfill even the slightest detail of is syntactic expectations), then we have a "bad sentence." Syntax is an "all or nothing" proposition. There is no gray area between correct and incorrect sentences. They are either right or wrong.

Syntactic Tree Diagrams

The syntactic trees developed more than 40 years ago do the best and most efficient job of portraying the interplay of constituents within a sentence. The much older Reed & Kellogg sentence diagramming of the 19th century gave us a good beginning, but they were completely incapable of showing the all-important hierarchies at work among the constituents of a sentence.

Syntax is at work on several levels of hierarchy within a sentence. The following tree diagram depicts the syntax at work within a prepositional phrase only:

"in a psychological sense"

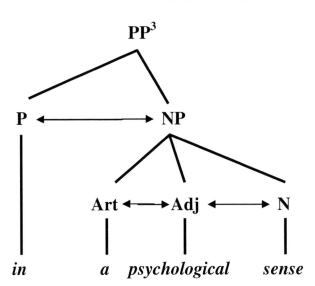

The hierarchies shown here are essential. The words in the noun phrase, *a psychological sense,* exhibit syntax at work on the most basic level of the sentence. Here the glue is working in a localized way to make a whole unit which, once made successfully, can interact on a higher level with the preposition. It cannot do this until the noun phrase is complete and has "jelled." The article, the adjective and the noun all relate to each other to satisfy the requirements of English

---

[3] Please see the following pages for definitions of these abbreviations.

46

grammar. Once jelled, the noun phrase is now ready to interact grammatically, and more powerfully with the preposition on a higher level, and we have the end result: *in a psychological sense.* The grammatical energy, the glue, the syntactic cohesion occurs on a higher level between the **P** and the **NP**. This entire prepositional phrase is a new constituent. In isolation, it just sits there, but if we want to use this prepositional phrase in the larger sentence as an adverb, the **PP** is now fully equipped and self-contained to be ready and available for such a function at a higher and more powerful level.

She helped us in a psychological sense.

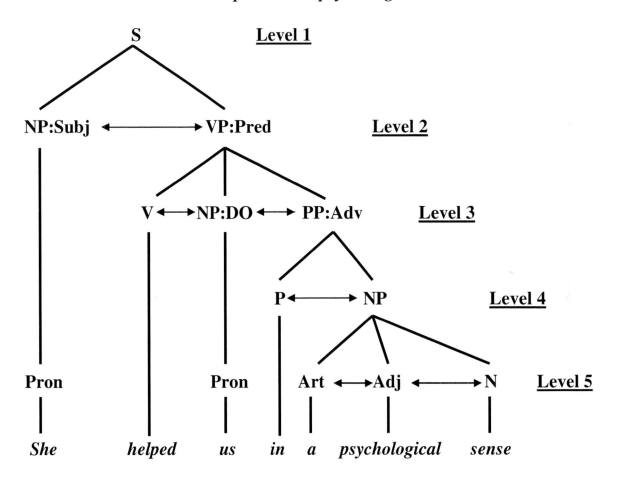

Notice the arrows occurring between constituents at each level. This is where the actual grammar (cohesion, syntax, or "glue") takes place, and it takes place in a clear hierarchy. The higher levels in the tree dominate the levels below. In order for the whole structure to work, each lower level (with its higher number) must jell grammatically for that grouping to qualify as a constituent for a higher level grouping. This, in turn, takes place on up the hierarchy so that each higher level constituent is a more general grouping made up of its lower level "children" constituents.

The constituents on a given level are called **sisters:** three on level 5 (**Art, Adj, N**), two on level 4 (**P, NP**), three on level 3 (**V, NP:DO, PP**) and three on level 2 (**NP, Aux, VP**). This is where the "glue" is being applied. The cohesive force of syntax works in these localized, hierarchical ways throughout the structure of a sentence.

In order for this to make sense, we must start at the lowest level to view the syntactic cohesion at work. We can't work up the tree until each lower level is syntactically complete.

Level 5

As described on the previous page, the grammatical action is taking place between the **Art**, the **Adj** and the **N**. Each one is capable of applying or receiving grammatical cohesion at this level. Therefore, the **Art** (a kind of adjective) and the **Adj** apply to the **N.**

Level 4

Most Common Constituents and their Abbreviations

Adj	Adjective
AdjClause	Adjective clause
AdjIdiom	Idiom being used as an adjective
Adv	Adverb
AdvClause	Adverb Clause
Art	Article
Aux	Auxiliary
Conj	Conjunction
DO	Direct Object
MV	Main Verb
N	Noun
NClause	Noun Clause
NP	Noun Phrase
P	Preposition
Part	Participle
PossPron	Possessive Pronoun
PP	Prepositional Phrase
Pred	Predicate
Pron	Pronoun
S	Sentence
Sub	Subordinator
Subj	Subject
V	Verb
VP	Verb Phrase

These three work on each other to produce a more generalized constituent, the **NP**, which is now capable of interacting with the **P**. Notice that the **P** does not interact individually with the 3 constituents on the lower level. It only interacts with the total grouping, now called an **NP.**

Level 3

These two, in turn, now form a new constituent, the **PP**, which is capable of interacting grammatically with the **NP:DO** and the **V.** The **V** does its work as a transitive verb applying direct action onto the **NP**, a direct object. Likewise, the entire **PP** does its grammatical work on this level to serve as an adverb modifying the **V**.

Level 2

Now the **VP** is complete. All of the cohesive potentials of the lower levels have passed their tests for the grammar of English, and the **VP** (the predicate) is fully capable of interacting on Level 2 with its counterpart, the **NP** (the subject of the sentence).

Level 1

The **S** is also a constituent. It is the seal of approval, the completed sentence in which all levels are functioning as they should.

Traditionally, we have tended to pay only scant attention to Levels 2, 3 and 4. These tree diagrams are capable of identifying and clarifying the detailed interaction among these all-important **middle managers** of a sentence.

The following sentence can serve as a model for learning and experimentation in the classroom. We recommend putting a tree diagram with a sentence like this up on the wall and leaving it there throughout the year. Near the diagram put large felt "semantic pockets" (described in the following chapter) into which students can add verbs, nouns, adjectives, etc. The constant reminder with this graphic depiction of the deep structure of English will build a foundation in the student's mind for the genuine, inner workings of the language.

The smart girl grabbed the screaming baby.

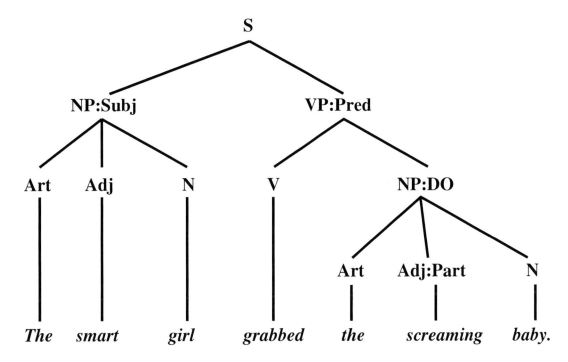

Variations: 1. Present this tree to students[4] with the adjectives missing and have them come up with suggestions:[5]

The _____ girl   grabbed   the   _____   baby.

2. With the nouns missing:

The   smart   _____   grabbed   the   screaming   _____.

3. With the verb missing:

The   smart   girl   _____   the   screaming   baby.

---

[4] We have found that children as young as 3rd graders love an exercise like this. The more constituents they can invent for a sentence such as this, the deeper will be their understanding of English grammar. Seeing hundreds of possibilities for new adjectives, nouns and verbs in a sentence structure like this will reinforce their grasp of the deepest levels of English grammar. It is this type of understanding, rather than rote learning of final forms of sentences, that will give them a genuine command of English.

[5] Have advanced students alternate between regular adjectives for the *baby* such as *little, happy, cute,* etc. and participles such as the one presented: *cooing, frightened, brown-eyed,* etc. It would be very instructive to take students through the morphological journey of verbs transforming into adjectives (participles).

Test Your Knowledge (Exercise 9)
"In the shaded corner"

Each of the following words and phrases could be used as constituents of a sentence. Name the syntactic category (part of speech) for each one of these constituents:

in:

the:

shaded:

corner:

the shaded corner:

in the shaded corner:

Using this prepositional phrase (*in the shaded corner*), make 2 different sentences where this PP functions:1. as an adjective, and 2. as an adverb:

1.

2.

Subordinate Clauses as Constituents in Sentences

One of the most powerful ways that languages interweave thoughts together is to embed one sentence (or more) into another sentence. When this happens, the subordinate or dependent "clause" (the sentence being **embedded**), becomes a **constituent** along with all the other constituents of the main sentence. In this capacity it functions exactly like other constituents. So, whole sentences can become **nouns, adjectives** or **adverbs**, functioning just as other single-word nouns adjectives or adverbs. The realization of this gives us another reason why traditional grammar terms are inadequate. In cases like these, since the subordinate clause will always contain a "subject," the "predicate" also includes a "subject;" or the "subject" may contain a "predicate." These older terms leave us confused. A better label is Noun Phrase, a more general description that fits the reality of a sentence.

This is another very important aspect of the **middle management** aspect of the intermediate levels of hierarchical control within a sentence. In the middle levels of the sentence hierarchy these embedded sentences "subordinate" themselves to the overall grammatical structure so that they can fit in on a particular level of grammatical control.

The following embedded sentences or subordinate clauses are **nouns**.

*She knew **that he bought the book.***
***That the election was rigged** became clear.*

*She knew **that he bought the book.***

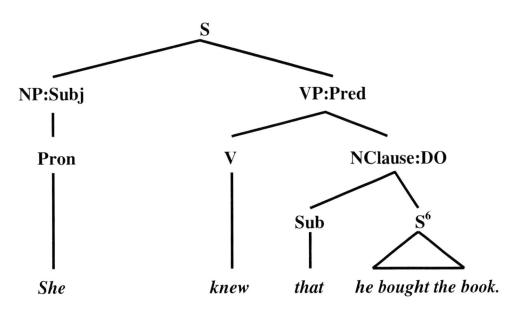

---

[6] Please note that a triangle can be used for a more compact use of space to designate a whole sentence as a constituent of the main clause.

The following subordinate clause is an **adjective** (These are also called **relative clauses**):

*He bought the book **that was on the bottom shelf.***

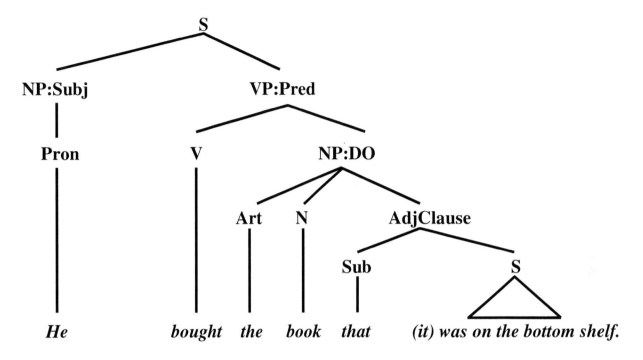

Here is a subordinate clause being used as an **adverb**:

*He will read it **when he is ready.***

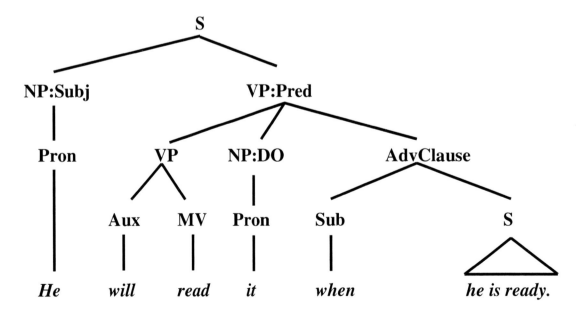

Deep Structure and its Surface Manifestations

The last five tree diagrams depict the **surface manifestations** of **deep structure** sentences. They are all in the declarative (indicative) mood, and in them the verb sits on its throne in the middle of its "court" (the rest of the sentence), unencumbered, regal and fully in control. These are the "couch potato" versions of a sentence. They could be in the imperative or the subjunctive mood as well as the declarative.

The trees themselves are a depiction of the grammatical order and control (the **deep structure**) we attach to visions, concepts, ideas and thoughts. We take the thought, break it up into its constituent parts (words and phrases), arrange a syntactic tree in our minds with all of the checks and balances it needs to fit the grammar of English, plug in the English words to unite the thought with the proper structure and release it all from our mouths as a finished sentence. If all the checks and balances are met, we declare this to be a good English sentence. If even a small unit misfires, it is a bad English sentence.

More than 40 years ago Noam Chomsky threw a monkey wrench into the study of linguistics. The behaviorists who preceded him believed that, in the spirit of pure science, we should consider language to be entirely a result of stimulus and response. They felt that a human being was essentially born with a clean slate containing no specific language information. According to them, children and all adults later would only reproduce the language as they heard it from other speakers without adding anything creative themselves. With that limitation in mind, Chomsky challenged them to explain how it is, then, that all human beings, even children, can come up with sentences that have never been said before.[7] The behaviorists had no answer.

Chomsky maintained that humans carry within their brains an innate set of templates for language; he called it a **LAD (language acquisition device).** These templates are sitting there in a baby's brain, waiting to be filled with the nuts and bolts of language. They seem to be born with the rudiments of grammar. Essentially these are grammatical expectations, and the adults in the baby's life provide all of the forms of language, from words to full sentences to meet those expectations. Examples of these rudiments are **phonemes, morphemes, content**

---

[7] Ask yourself as you go through this course how many new sentences you have heard during class, or how many have you created yourself. Anyone can easily produce sentences that have never been heard before by any human being.

words and **function words** along with **sentence patterns.** From their native tongue the adults will provide examples for all of these and will reinforce the outlines of syntactic trees which the baby also already has in template form.

This transference of linguistic aptitude is nothing short of miraculous, especially when one considers that a child's parents do not give the child anything close to consistency when delivering the language. When a child comes up with a sentence never heard before, this can only happen if the child already has a syntactic tree in his or her mind sitting there, waiting for the blanks (words) to be filled in. **These very trees <u>are</u> the deep structure** (Pinker 1994:121). A child or an adult, or especially a poet, simply plug new words into these trees.

Ambiguity is more "proof" of the deep structure of sentences. In the following example sentence, we are looking at one surface manifestation for two different deep structures (Fromkin 2003:143-144). Presented in isolation, one cannot tell whether the boy or the man has the telescope. Of course, if this were the fourth or fifth sentence of an opening paragraph, it would be clear who has the telescope, but in isolation there is simply no way to tell. The deep structure, the tree, is more reliable than the surface structure. In both of these sentences the middle levels of grammar are crucial to the understanding of the ambiguity. The issue is the role of the prepositional phrase.

The boy saw the man with the telescope.
(The boy is holding the telescope.)

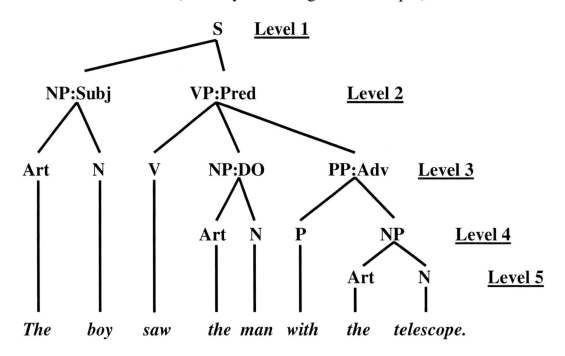

In this case, the **PP** is on Level 3. It is higher than its position in the following example and is, therefore, capable of working grammatically on the level of the **V**. It is an adverb modifying the verb telling us how the boy saw the man. With this tree diagram the **PP** can only be an adverb. It is too high in the hierarchy to modify the noun *man*. Each constituent works wherever it can on its own level and not on any other level. This tree shows clearly that it is the boy who is holding the telescope and is viewing the man.

Not so in the following sentence:

The boy saw the man with the telescope.
(The man has the telescope.)

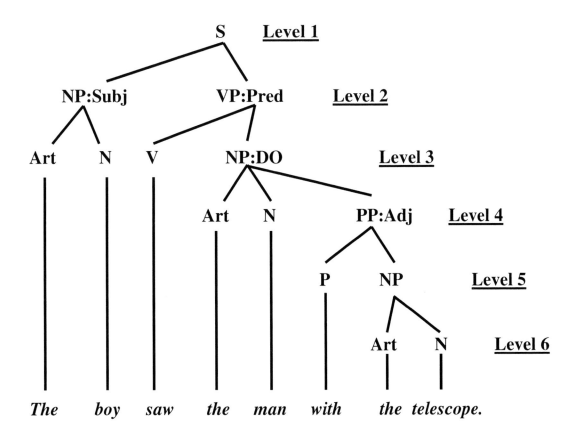

In this case, the **PP** is on Level 4 and is totally incapable of modifying the verb now; it is too low for that. It is on the level with the noun *man*. This makes the entire prepositional phrase an adjective modifying *man*. We could say this another way, "The boy saw the man who was holding the telescope." Level 3 now is left alone for only two constituents to interact with each other (the verb and the noun phrase). This tree, also, completely disambiguates the sentence.

Try to put this explanation in your own words and then teach this to another teacher, a friend, or even your students. The more you can clarify what is going on here, the better will be your students' understanding of the grammar. What is remarkable is that we already knew all of this before we even saw this sentence and its trees. We have these trees buried deep within our brains, and we constantly bring them out to produce new sentences.

Transformations and their Surface Manifestations

The interaction between **deep structure** sentences and their **transformations** has been a major part of linguistics ever since Chomsky introduced the concept in the middle of the last century. The deep structure of a sentence is not a finished product coming out of a speaker's mouth. It is more a conceptualization in a speaker's mind of what he or she wants to say. Steven Pinker (see below) says that the deep structure is the tree itself without any words attached to it yet. That conceptualization is the thought to be expressed, joined, in rudimentary form, with expectations of what a human sentence should look like in general grammatical terms.

Deep structure: This refers to a basic assumption in Chomskian linguistics that all sentences in human communication stem from a complete thought in its "neutral state." They might be in the indicative (declarative), imperative or subjunctive mood, but they would not be passive or interrogative. Each "deep structure" sentence is in its "natural" or "untampered" state, in its basic subject – verb – object (**SVO**) formation (for English) and without any particular element being singled out for emphasis.
Transformations, on the other hand, exhibit some type of "tampering" with the basic sentence. As examples of this overall assumption, all questions, all passive sentences and all sentences in which any constituent is singled out for emphasis and is, therefore, moved to some "unnatural" position in the sentence, are transformations. They "come from" the deep structure version and become new sentences by one of four processes: **deletion**, **addition**, **movement** or **alteration** involving some element of the deep structure sentence.

Once the speaker has the thought in mind, the basic structure with which to form the thought and the correct language to insert it into, then he or she produces a **surface manifestation** of the deep structure sentence or its transformation. All of this happens in a tiny fraction of a second. If speaker's "default" language is English, then all of the phonological, morphological and semantic expectations of English fall automatically upon the deep structure of the thought, the speaker's mind coordinates all of the requirements of what an English sentence should sound like, and the speaker releases the full sentence in the shining glory of a proper English sentence. That is the surface manifestation.

All of the sentences on the left are surface manifestations of deep structure, and all on the right are surface manifestations of transformations:

Deep structure	**Transformations**
Braden jammed the toy forcefully.	Braden forcefully jammed the toy. (movement)
	Forcefully Braden jammed the toy. (movement)
Logan pinched Braden.	Braden was pinched by Logan. (movement & addition)
I know that Lilly was sleeping.	I know Lilly was sleeping. (deletion)
Landon is working.	Is Landon working? (movement)
Landon loves to work.	Does Landon love to work? (addition & deletion)
Landon has to work.	Does Landon have to work? (addition & alteration)

What does this mean? The premise for this dichotomy is that anytime you move phrases around in a sentence that deviate from the "normal" word order, anytime you change the voice of a sentence from active to passive, and anytime you form a question, you are "transforming" the neutral, declarative concept represented in the deep structure. When you move *forcefully* from its final position to any position earlier in the sentence, you have made a transformation, perhaps to use the adverbial energy to emphasize a different part of the sentence.

Whenever you turn an active sentence into a passive one, you are altering the deep structure for some effect, perhaps to diminish the importance of the doer of the

---

Transformations involve changes in sentences such as:

Movement: Moving a word, such as the adverb *forcefully* in the 1st two examples above, from its more neutral position after the verb to an earlier position in the sentence. This can be used for a different emphasis.

Addition: Adding words, *was* and *by* above, in order to turn an active sentence into the passive.

Deletion: Removing words, such as the subordinator *that* in the sentence above, for a more efficient expression of the thought. When a sentence contains a number of subordinate clauses, the writer must be careful not to lose clarity by the removal of too many subordinators.

Alteration: In the last example above, in order to form a question, not only do we need to add the auxiliary *does*, but we must also change the modal auxiliary from *has to* (an idiom) to *have to* since the separated auxiliary *does* now carries the inflectional morpheme –*s* for the 3rd person singular form of the verb.

58

action, to emphasize the recipient of the action or even to remove awareness of the doer altogether.[8] Whenever you turn a declarative sentence into a question, you are transforming the deep structure.

Seldom does one have the liberty of making sweeping generalizations about language, but in these cases it works: All passive sentences and all questions are transformations of deep structure sentences.

The convention for showing a transformation in a tree diagram is to leave the space of the moved element blank and to add an arrow under the diagram to show the new location of the element in the transformed sentence as shown here:

Surface manifestation
of deep structure:

Surface manifestation
of a transformation:

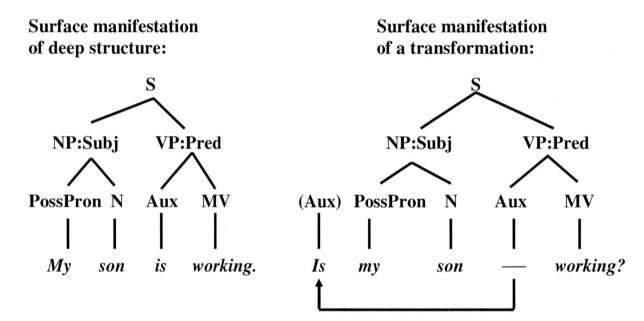

---

[8] When Ronald Reagan said, "Mistakes were made" (December 6, 1986 on the "Iran-Contra Affair"), he removed his or anyone else's accountability from the action. Politicians would be hard pressed if they could not resort to the passive voice.

What follows is a visual depiction of how we produce the surface manifestations of deep structure sentences or of transformations.

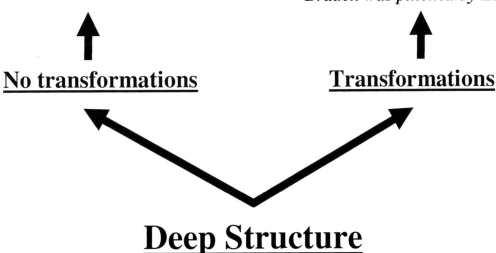

Surface structure manifestation of the deep structure:

Braden jammed the toy forcefully.

Logan pinched Braden.

Surface structure manifestation of the transformations:

Braden forcefully jammed the toy.
Did Braden jam the toy forcefully?

Did Logan pinch Braden?
Braden was pinched by Logan.

No transformations

Transformations

Deep Structure

Deep structure is a primitive form of the tree itself without any words. It is "the interface between the mental dictionary [lexicon] and the phrase structure" (Pinker 1994:121). If the language chosen is English, it must conform to the English expectations of SVO word order and grammar. Most deep structure sentences are in the declarative (indicative), imperative or subjunctive mood and in the active voice. They are in their "statement form" (generally with a period at the end), not their "question form." The vast majority are "plain, old statements" in a neutral word order. At this level the verb gets everything it wants. Its retinue, both before and after, is all in order, none in rebellion; the verb sits there on its throne, unencumbered and regal.

Test Your Knowledge (Exercise 10)
"The X-ray vision of a sentence"

Make a syntactic tree and develop your grammatical
X-ray vision of this sentence:

Smart kids eat broccoli.

Test Your Knowledge (Exercise 11)
"Sentences within sentences"

Articulate the syntactic roles of the following embedded clauses. They are also called dependent or subordinate clauses (They were full sentences before they became subordinated to the main clause). Grammatically "visualize" them as constituents in these sentences. Provide brief explanations about what you "see:"

A. Adjective or noun?

1. *I see the man **who is standing in the shaded corner.***
2. *I can't see **who is standing in the shaded corner.***

B. Noun or adverb?

1. ***If it rains tomorrow,** we will have to stay home.*
2. *We don't know **if it is going to rain tomorrow or not.***
3. ***Whether it rains tomorrow or not,** we are going to John Muir Woods.*

Now that you know about morphemes, lexical gaps and syntactic structures, try your hand at a classroom exercise such as the following:

"The Wozy Briggles"

The	wozy	briggles	have	been	blimming	vorefully	in	the	biddybam
(white)	(green)	(blue)	(white)	(white)	(red)	(yellow)	(white)	(white)	(blue)

.		**?**
(white)		(white)

[Cut up cards from white, green, blue, red and yellow cardboard as shown above. The card with "blimming" written on it should measure about 14 in. by 4 in. Make the others in proportion to this. Print the words with large black markers so that they can be easily read by students at the back of the room. Write four of the cards in both lower and upper case on each side: *The/the, The/the, In/in,* and *Have/have.* The white cards are for function words; the colored ones are for content words. Notice that only the content words (nouns, verbs, adjectives and adverbs) have the flexibility to become "lexical gaps." The function words have no equivalent sense of humor. The four colors, other than white, are often sold together in large cardboard sheets.]

1. Ask for 12 volunteers from your class.
2. Bring them to the front of the class, giving each one a card.
3. Tell them to do whatever comes to their minds about them.
4. As the 10 volunteers with the words are negotiating about what to do, take the two with the period and the question mark aside. Tell the person with the period to observe the sentence in formation and to show up at the end of the sentence only when the sentence is grammatically acceptable. Tell the person with the question mark to wait until we transform the sentence into a question.
5. If the sentence is acceptable but in an order other than seen above, have the person with the main verb ("blimming") command the relevant cards to go to the positions shown above. The main verb is the "Queen" or "King" of the sentence and has the power to order the members of his/her "court" around. The order shown above is a surface manifestation of this sentence in its "deep structure."

6. **Transform this declarative sentence:**

   a. Have "vorefully" move into as many positions as would be grammatically acceptable and discuss the ways this movement alters the meaning of the sentence.

   b. Ask the rest of the students in the class whether the prepositional phrase ("in the biddybam") is functioning as an adjective or an adverb in the sentence.

   c. Tell the three people holding this prepositional phrase to leave their positions and to move as a group along the

      sentence to see if anyone will let them into a new position.

   d. With the PP in the front of the sentence, ask the class whether it is functioning as an adverb or an adjective.

   e. With the PP just after "briggles" (now reading "The wozy briggles in the biddybam"), ask the class the same question. All of these changes are transformations.

   f. Rearrange ("transform") the word order to make this sentence a question.

   g. Now the period moves away and the person with the question mark appears at the end of the sentence. Make sure that the first word of the sentence is in upper case.

   h. With each transformation, make sure that the first word of the sentence is in upper case.

7. With each transformation have students discuss the syntactic roles of each of the constituents that have been moved. Especially have students think about the "middle managers" of the sentence and the ways they influence each other.

8. Explore any other transformational possibilities. The students will enjoy moving around to see just how far they can take this rearranging of English word order.

9. Ask the students what the sentence means. The lexical gaps are "asking for meaning to be assigned them." You will find that some will become attached to meanings they have assigned to some of the words. This process will reinforce students' realization of the power of linguistic fusion between sound and meaning.

10. This exercise will also reinforce students' awareness of the sentence order patterns (the "tree structures") they already have in their minds.

11. We have found that students from 3rd grade onward will thrive with sentences such as this. If the lexical gaps are too much for your younger students, write real English words on the backs of the cards.

12. Or, have students come up with their own lexical gaps to replace these.

Chapter 4

Semantics: The World of Meaning

If we were to remove the world of meaning from language, there would be no language whatsoever. Sounds made by the human voice must be fused with meaning or the sounds have no purpose. Does this mean that all sounds have meaning? No, but all human voice sounds used for the purpose of communication have meaning from the most rudimentary, individual sounds to the longest discourse[1]. The vast majority of sounds chosen for meaning are entirely **arbitrary.** This means that there is no inherent connection between the sounds and their meaning; there is no "reason" why certain sounds stand for certain meaning. All of the following words mean "house" in several languages:

English	*house*
Spanish	*casa*
French	*maison*
German	*Haus*
Greek	*spiti*
Turkish	*ev*
Dutch	*huis*

> **Arbitrary**: For most words there is no connection between the meaning and the sound of a word.
> That is not the case with **onomatopoeia** [Greek: "to make a name"]. The sounds of words like *buzz* and *splash* imitate the physical process being defined.

Clearly there is a relationship between the Dutch, German and English versions. That is because about 2,500 years ago, these three were one and the same language, and these three words have diverged only a little in that time. Nevertheless, none of these three languages can provide any reason why we say [haus] for that type of building. It is simply an assignment of sound to meaning. All languages must do this in order to have a large enough vocabulary to communicate complete thoughts. The only words in which one could say that sound and meaning are united are the words of **onomatopoeia** such as *bow-wow, splash, bang,* etc. They take their sounds from the physical process being described.

---

[1] Remember that linguistics has nothing to do with writing. It focuses exclusively on the spoken language.

Meaning is involved at all levels:

Phonology	a phoneme /t/
	its allophones: [t, ɾ, tʰ, ʔ]²
Morphology	*book* (a morpheme and a word)
	-s (a morpheme)
Syntax	*in the book* (a prepositional phrase)
	There were many fascinating episodes
	in the book (a sentence).
	a paragraph
	a paper
	a poem
	a novel

Phonemes and their allophones don't have full meaning as such, but they signal meaning; that is to say, they are the building blocks for a string of sounds (morphemes and words) which do have full meaning. There are a few exceptions to this; for example, the word *Oh!* is a phoneme, a morpheme, a word and a complete thought (a "sentence" of sorts) all in one.

Does the *–s* at the end of *books* have meaning? Yes, but not in the full sense that a word has meaning. Its meaning can only emerge in attached dependence at the end of nouns to make them plural.

As we saw in the last chapter, *in the book* carries meaning as a grouping which the individual words themselves do not possess. It can be an adjective or an adverb depending on the syntactic expectations of the sentence into which it fits.

One of the best ways to gain a deeper understanding of the meaning of a word is to explore its **etymology** [Greek: "the study of the true sense of a word"]. This provides one of the best ways for students to deepen their understanding of vocabulary. Invariably, looking at the origin of the morphemes of a word gives the learner a totally new perspective about its modern usage. When your students use a dictionary, encourage them to linger a while as they look up a word so that they can absorb these deeper meanings.

---

² We will learn about these in the following two chapters.

"Semantic Pockets" in our Lexicons

What does the organization of vocabulary in our "mental dictionaries" (our **lexicons**[3]) look like? No one can say for sure, but there is no question that our brains have ways of organizing the world of meaning we carry for the languages we speak.

One way to visualize this is to think of the stacks of books in a library. Let's say that an educated native speaker of English has control of about 60,000 words. We know by the examples shown in Broca's Aphasia vs. Wernicke's Aphasia (pages 36 and following in the Fromkin book), that we store **function words** and **content words** in different parts of the brain. This is undoubtedly the most basic division of vocabulary. As to content words, it is also clear that we have ways of storing them in groups, all the way from large groups of content words (e.g., nouns, verbs, adjectives and adverbs) to small groups (e.g., colors, musical instruments, etc.). Bibliographers in a library have to make decisions as to which grouping a particular book should belong. The main disciplines of a university provide an obvious basis for the groupings. Also, books attached to a particular language will be a criterion. Inevitably, compromises will have to be reached because millions of books belong in more than one category. There is no perfect way to store all of the books in the stacks so that they will fit all relevant criteria. In like manner, words may belong to a particular category but may also belong to many other categories outside the main one.

> **Lexicon** [Greek: "wordbook"]: the "dictionary" in our brains, i.e., one's "mental dictionary." **Dictionary** (from Latin): the actual reference book with words organized alphabetically.

> **Content words:** Nouns, verbs, adjectives and adverbs, the words which are loaded with meaning but have a minimum of grammar. They are an **open class**, receptive to new members such as lexical gaps and new coinages.
> **Function words**: Prepositions, conjunctions, pronouns, articles, auxiliaries & subordinators. They are a **closed class**, entirely unreceptive to new additions.

Another metaphor might be the use of general to specific "menus" in a computer. This can have the advantage of showing groupings within groupings.

---

[3] One of the remarkable features of English is its ability to borrow words from all languages and adapt them to meet specific needs. English conveniently takes the Latin version of this concept to stand for the physical book and the Greek version for the mental one.

As is so often the case in the study of language, it is a metaphor that is most useful in helping us to visualize and then to organize and teach word groupings around meaning: **semantic pockets** (pockets within pockets within pockets).

It would seem that our brains have an ability to organize these pockets in several different locations with many ways to have them overlap and interact. Some pockets are far removed from each other. Others are close together. A word may belong to many different pockets at the same time, as is depicted in the graph below. The word "noun" is the **hypernym** (the general term) for all of the **hyponyms** (all of the individual words "under" this category) contained in the pocket. All words in English can be designated as either hypernyms or hyponyms. The hypernym **noun** subsumes all of the many thousands of its hyponyms, that is, all of the "persons, places, things, ideas" and even "sentences within sentences" (noun clauses which serve as subjects or direct objects for the main clause). The two-word hypernym, **musical instruments,** stands for the specific categories listed among its hyponyms, such as clarinet, trumpet, etc. This is an example where English simply does not have a single word to serve as the hypernym.

Hypernyms

Hyponyms

These two categories make up the entire lexicon of any language.

Nouns

At least 200,000 in English

Musical Instruments

Clarinet	Violin
Trumpet	Viola
Flute	Piccolo
Oboe	Timpani
Trombone	Bass
Cello	Horn
Piano	Tuba

Or, a single pocket may contain groups that completely oppose each other, such as **antonyms:**

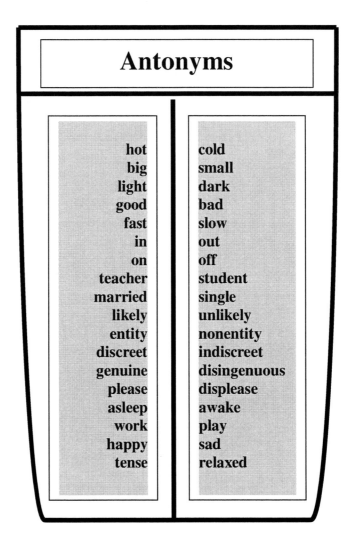

Antonyms	
hot	cold
big	small
light	dark
good	bad
fast	slow
in	out
on	off
teacher	student
married	single
likely	unlikely
entity	nonentity
discreet	indiscreet
genuine	disingenuous
please	displease
asleep	awake
work	play
happy	sad
tense	relaxed

Word opposites appear to be connected like "toggle switches" such that going back and forth between them requires almost no effort for our brains.

Put these "pockets" up in your classroom and leave them there all year long. You can make these cheaply out of felt (An ideal size is about 13" x 16"). We have found that it is useful to separate all content words from all function words. Use the same colors[4] as shown in the "Wozy Briggles:" red for verbs, blue for nouns,

---

[4] The choice of color really doesn't matter. We make these suggestions for two reasons: 1. Usually these four are sold together and are, therefore, cheaper than specialized colors; and 2. Of these four red is often associated with aggressiveness, and this is appropriate for verbs. The important thing is to pick a set and stay with it for your cards, pockets, etc.

green for adjectives and yellow for adverbs. Be sure to put a sign at the top of each pocket for the **hypernym.**

We suggest putting the function words in white felt pockets. It would be useful to have one of these be devoted to the prepositions. Here are most of the common single-word prepositions[5] in English (Thurman 2002:82; Celce-Murcia & Larsen-Freeman 1999:401-424; Hopper 2000:30-32):

aboard	behind	down	onto	under
about	below	during	out	underneath
above	beneath	except	outside	until
across	beside	for	over	up
after	between	from	past	upon
against	beyond	in	regarding	with
along	but	inside	since	within
among	by	into	than	without
around	concerning	like	through	
as	considering	of	throughout	
at	despite	off	to	
before	down	on	toward	

This closed group of function words is so powerful in English that it is good for students to have a grasp of them as a whole. Also, it is just the right size to "fill a pocket."

Teaching the *-nyms* to Stimulate Metacognitive Learning

The *–nyms* provide a perfect example of the productive use of morphemes to gain leverage in the building of vocabulary. A good dictionary will provide a full entry for this suffix, *-onym* [Greek: having a specified kind of name]. Learning the prefix along with this morpheme gives students depth in their understanding. We suggest that you have your students learn the literal meanings of these words first as you see them on the next page in the square brackets of the shaded boxes.

When teaching any aspect of the grammar of English, it is important for educators to see the 'whole picture" of what is necessary for students to gain control of the language. If you give a few **antonyms** in a given lesson, be sure that you have in mind the teaching of more than one or two. Once you have their attention with words such as *big/small, bright/dim,* etc., don't just give these examples in

---

[5] Other common prepositions with more than one word are: *according to, because of, in back of, in front of, in spite of, on top of, out of, next to, speaking of, together with, along with, with respect to* and *with regard to.*

isolation. If that particular moment in a unit is not appropriate for expansion, find a time when you can expand with antonyms to give them a full list of forty to fifty. What is the purpose of this?

Antonym ["opposite name"]: A second word with a meaning opposite to the first one, *big/small, high/low*
Heteronym ["different name"]: Words spelled the same but pronounced differently for different meanings, *wind, dove, bass, row.*
Homonym ["same name"]: Different words that are pronounced the same but are not spelled the same. "Homonym" is a synonym to **homophone** ["same sound"].
They're/their/there, bear/bare, read/red are both homonyms and homophones.
Hypernym ["over name"]: All words belong to a category larger than themselves; this is the term for that larger category. A *cat* is one member of the hypernym *animal.*
Hyponym ["under name"]: all of the members of a hypernym category. All cats and all animals are "under names" for the hypernym *noun.*
Metonym ["named afterwards"]. After a period of time some specific words, often physical objects, become associated so deeply with a larger concept that they become the name for that more general concept: *brass* for military leaders, *Pentagon* for the American military establishment, *crown* for a monarch. *Bureau* has gone through many metonymic changes from its earlier French meaning, "cloth cover for desks."
Retronym ["named backwards;" this is the only *–nym* on this list with a Latin morpheme.] These expressions would not have made sense when the original concept was created. At first baseball was only played during the day; there would have been no point in calling it *day baseball.* Others are *acoustic guitar, bar soap, snail mail, straight razor.*
Synonym ["named together"]: These are the words of a thesaurus, close enough to each other in meaning to be considered a "family" of words: *bright, brilliant, radiant, lustrous.* A good dictionary will include these.

Throughout your teaching, one of your major objectives must always be to provide a large enough paradigm of a particular linguistic feature of English so that all students "get it." That is to say, they must receive enough reinforcement from you of the language patterns they already have in their minds so that the language structure becomes enhanced and powerful enough that they can become aware of "what they know but don't yet know that they know." Your filling out of a paradigm such as antonyms stimulates students to bring these groupings closer to the surface, into their conscious minds. That is how they can begin to become "airborne" with the language. This is how they can begin to develop **metacognitive** skills so that they can manage their own learning processes throughout their lives.

This list of *–nyms* may be more than you will ever present to your students. Depending on the age and abilities of your students, perhaps only three or four of them would be appropriate. Certainly you should include **antonyms, homonyms** and **synonyms.**

On the other hand, it may not be enough. Perhaps students of high school age or older will become inspired by the concept of the *–nyms* and carry it to an extreme. Having students bring some research into the classroom to teach more of these forms will certainly enhance their metacognitive skills. There is no better way to learn something than to teach it. We strongly encourage you to have your students teach portions of the material of your course.

Homonyms or **homophones** are important, and they can be a lot of fun to teach. In fact, they need to be done with a light heart, precisely because they help to make up the "trickery" of the relationship between the sounds of English and its writing system. This trickery can become a disturbing stumbling block for students, and they need the humor to get through.

Here is an example for older learners:

> *Wood you believe that I didn't no*
> *About homophones until too daze ago?*
> *That day in hour class in groups of for,*
> *We had to come up with won or more.*
>
> *Mary new six; enough to pass,*
> *But my ate homophones lead the class.*
> *Then a thought ran threw my head,*
> *"Urn a living from homophones," it said.*
>
> *I guess I just sat and staired into space.*
> *My hole life seamed to fall into place.*
> *Our school's principle happened to come buy,*
> *And asked about the look in my I.*
>
> *"Sir," said I as bowled as could bee,*
> *"My future rode I clearly sea."*
> *"Sun," said he, 'move write ahead,*
> *Set sail on your coarse. Don't be misled."*
>
> *I herd that gnus with grate delight.*
> *I will study homophones both day and knight.*
> *For weaks and months, through thick oar thin,*
> *I'll pursue my goal. Eye no aisle win.*

(By George E. Coon, from "The Reading Teacher," April, 1976)

Metaphors

Metaphors are **"semantic earthquakes."** Here we are using another metaphor to define this term. Metaphors seem to come out of nowhere, and they are very striking when one sees them for the first time. Why is this the case? What is happening when we encounter expressions such as:

*My car is a **lemon**.*
*Tell me the **story** of your life.*
*Universities are **incubators** for new ideas.*
*Noam Chomsky is the **father** of modern linguistics.*
*I can't **take my eyes off** her (This is also an idiom. In such cases the metaphor is buried into a phrase where the grammatical relationship between the words is neither normal, predictable nor literal. This abnormality of grammar is what makes the phrase an idiom).*
*Let me put in my **two cents' worth**.*
*His whole life **revolves** around her.*
*That was a **cutting** remark.*
*This is a **budding** theory.*
*We need to **stew** over that for a while.*
*She is at the **height** of her power.*
*Your words seem **hollow**.*
*He had a **full** life.*
*She's **brimming** with vim and vigor.*
*That **blew me away** (also an idiom).*
*He doesn't have an **honest bone in his body** (also an idiom).*
*We could barely **contain our joy** (also an idiom).*
*She is a **knockout**.*
*His eyes were **filled** with sadness.*
*They have a **sick** relationship.*
*Let's make a syntactic **tree**.*
*His ideas aren't worth a **tinker's dam**.*

Metaphors are created when a vocabulary item from one semantic pocket is forced into a second semantic pocket that is located far away in our lexicons. Until the moment of creation these two pockets had nothing to do with each other. It is no mistake that poets are the best at creating metaphors. A good poet has enough linguistic flexibility to come up with the idea of using the power of an unrelated concept to strongly enhance the meaning of another concept. The juxtaposition of the two is so strong that it takes us by surprise. It can even shock the person hearing it for the first time; it is a semantic earthquake.

The definition of metaphor given by Lakoff and Johnson is instructive; it shows us that language is far more than just words. Culture is deeply buried within language, and one of the most powerful ways the members of a culture instill and reinforce its values is through metaphor. In their first chapter, "Concepts We Live By," they present a compelling line of reasoning that in our culture "ARGUMENT IS WAR" (Lakoff & Johnson 1980:4). This concept is deeply embedded in metaphors such as the following presented in this book:

> **Metaphor:** "The essence of metaphor is understanding and experiencing one kind of thing in terms of another." (Lakoff & Johnson 1980:5).
> **Simile:** A figure of speech comparing two dissimilar concepts, usually with the words *like* and *as, sharp as a tack, growing like a weed.*

*Your claims are **indefensible.***
*His claims were **right on target.***
*I **demolished** his argument.*
*You disagree? Okay, **shoot!***
*If you use that strategy, he'll **wipe you out.***
*He **shot down** all of my arguments.*

How are metaphors **semantic earthquakes?** When Dylan Thomas created the expression *a grief ago,* he forced together two semantic pockets which are far away from each in our lexicons. As is shown on the next page, *grief* belongs in a pocket whose hypernym is emotions, while *ago* belongs with time expressions. In their normal linguistic life these pockets have nearly nothing to do with each other, but with an expression like this their meanings are suddenly intermingled. At first hearing one is rather stunned in a pleasant way by the juxtaposition. It makes one stop to think about how there is, indeed, a kind of regularity to the periods of grief in our lives.

76

Metaphors as "Semantic Earthquakes"
Dylan Thomas's expression "*a grief ago*"

In this example, expressions of time suddenly "invade" expressions of emotion, and vice versa. As is true of good metaphors, the more one thinks about them, the better they become; these are the **aftershocks.** An adult can easily respond to such an expression by saying, "Yes, I can think of a certain regularity to the periods of grief in my life." Typically a very young child would not be able to relate to such a concept.

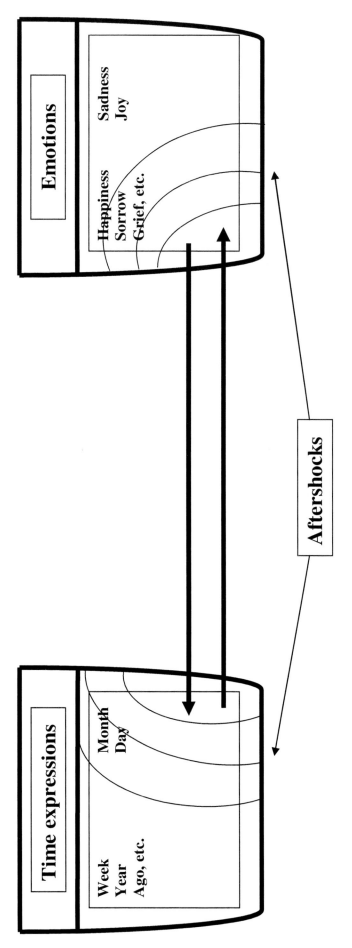

Metaphors are much stronger than **similes** in that a semantic distance is always preserved when one says "something is like something else." With metaphors the new concept becomes a part of an established semantic world. In a sense the invasion is permanent; both of these semantic pockets now contain "foreign" concepts which permanently influence and enrich their "new surroundings." One's culture and language seem to thrive and flourish by such enrichment. English would be poverty stricken if all of its metaphors were removed.

© 2008 by *Steven Landon West. All rights reserved.*
www.linguisticsforeducators.com

Idioms

It is impossible to overemphasize the importance of actively teaching **idioms** to ELs. They need to be introduced over and over throughout a learner's experience.

> **Idiom:** "a set phrase of two or more words that means something different from the literal meaning of the individual words" (Ammer 1997:preface).

Why is this the case? All languages have them, and this itself can be a challenge for an ESL or EFL student; translation might simply get such a student into trouble in the communication. Also, they are very common, occupying a primary position in all discourse. In addition, they are very fussy. Not only do they have to be uttered in precise word order and grammar; they must also be uttered with precisely the correct intonation to have proper impact in English. Otherwise, they fall flat. Adult ELs are often left out of a fast-moving conversation in English in which idioms are flying freely. They don't want to be left out, but they also know instinctively that it would be difficult to ask just what a given idiom means in the middle of a social dialogue. Look at the following list of traps for ELs:

> *It's raining **cats and dogs.***
> *You're **pulling my leg.***
> *We don't want to **miss the boat.***
> ***Bite your tongue!***
> *If that happens, I'll **eat my hat.***
> *Do you really think he is a competent president? **In a pig's eye!***
> *We plan to go **the whole nine yards** in this confirmation hearing.*
> *He believed everything she said, **hook, line and sinker.***
> *She broke out **in a cold sweat** when the police walked in.*
> *They cleaned out our house **lock, stock and barrel.***
> *Let's not **gild the lily** in this program.*
> *His boss **made him eat crow.***
> *We are going to **push the envelope.***

One of our students related the following story. She was babysitting a little girl one evening and was helping her with idioms. She taught her the meaning of the idiom *to pull my leg.* When the girl's parents came home later that evening, the little girl hid behind the sofa, rushed out to greet her mother, grabbed her by the leg and said, "Mommy, I'm pulling your leg."

Especially for young children and for adult ESL/EFL students, it is useful to "experience" these idioms literally as much as possible, just as did the little girl described above.

This provides an excellent opportunity for art teachers to "portray" idioms on paper. Children will never forget a work of art with "cats and dogs" on little clouds all over the sky.

Another good technique for children and adults is a game of charades in the teaching of idioms. Have one or two students come to the front of the class and act out the literal meaning of an idiom and have the class guess what it is.

We suggest that you teach at least 100 idioms throughout an academic year with adult EL's, and you need to return to these on a regular basis. This number will naturally be reduced for younger ELs.

Phrasal Verbs

Phrasal verbs are an extremely important aspect of idioms. They fit the definition of idioms in that the two or three elements of each verb are not normal; that is, the grammar holding these elements together is not normal. Verbs such as *do in, put up with, get up, take off, have at, run up, come on,* and many thousands of other examples in English do not contain prepositions.

> **"Phrasal verbs,** also called *two-word verbs,* are idiomatic expressions because the second element of the verb. . . is not necessarily predictable" (Spears 2005:v).

Those short words after the main verb are called **particles**.[6] Real prepositions, which these short words are in most other usages in the language, do, indeed, "preposit" the noun phrases they apply to: *in the corner, up the hill, with my friend, off the carpet, at the school,* and *on the table.* In these cases the prepositions are "normal," and the entire prepositional phrase functions as an adjective or an adverb, either describing a noun preceding the phrase or modifying the action in the verb.

---

[6] **Particles** are a sort of non-descript group of short words in English and in many other languages which "fill in" for localized grammar. In other languages (such as Turkish, Chinese and Japanese) they have more precise functions, such as turning a statement into a question or clarifying the precise "case" of a preceding word. For English it is difficult to pin down an exact definition. *To* is often used in English for such non-descript purposes: *to go* (and all other infinitives), *ought to, used to, have to, about to,* etc.

Phrasal verbs do no such thing. Rather than going before a noun phrase, their initial grammar works backward into the preceding verb, and they participate in a specialized meaning in which the verb phrase now acts as a whole verb applying its grammatical energy to the noun phrase following or standing alone as many intransitive verbs can do: *Even though they had a fight, the two **made up**.*

Traditional English grammars have essentially ignored phrasal verbs, pretending as if they contained prepositions but not really facing the reality which is that these are not prepositions at all, but something completely different. Because these short words look like prepositions, many ELs will be confused as to just what they are doing in English sentences. In addition, they are "all over the place" in their meaning and usage:

> *The two friends **made up** a story.*
> *They really **made** it **up**.*
> *Then, after their fight about just what the story should be **made up of**,*
> *   they **made up**.*

They have to be learned because they are so common in the language. *McGraw-Hill's Dictionary of American Idioms and Phrasal Verbs* by Richard A. Spears contains some 12,000 phrasal verbs for contemporary American English.

Test Your Knowledge (Exercise 12)
"The meaning of phrasal verbs"
A. Phrasal verbs are idioms. Prepare an explanation of this that would be meaningful to an EL, especially to one who is not familiar with the concept in their native tongue.

B. Describe the grammar (the cohesive relationship) between the two words in these phrasal verbs. Which way is the "glue flowing" in these examples, what is the new meaning of the phrase after it is glued together, and how does that new constituent (after it is glued together) function in the rest of the sentence? Are these verbs transitive or intransitive? Give examples:

♦ *take on*

♦ *take off*

♦ *take over*

Is it an idiom or a metaphor?

Idioms

- Must be two or more words
- The crucial difference is in the "abnormal" grammar of the phrase: *put up with.*
- Are esoteric and fussy. ELs often have difficulty understanding them as well as using them properly in a conversation. An EL was once overheard trying to use the phrase *son of a bitch,* but he ended up saying, *"Bitch baby!"*
- Thousands of idioms are phrasal verbs; they have specialized meaning emerging from the "abnormal" grammar between a verb and its particle: *look up.*

(Intersection)

- Both are very common.
- All languages have them.
- Many, but not all, idioms contain metaphors:

An idiom containing a metaphor: "He is *under the weather.*"

An idiom without a metaphor: "We're going to *look it up* in the dictionary." (This is a separable phrasal verb).

Metaphors

- Can be one or more words
- If two or more, the grammar of the phrase is normal.
- The result of at least two *semantic pockets* permanently "invading" each other
- By their creation, the semantic world of the language becomes enriched.
- Sometimes only a metaphor can clarify a concept or express it most efficiently: *syntactic trees; semantic earthquakes;* "We're in a *pickle;*" "My car's a *lemon.*"

Definitions

Metaphor

(AHD 2000): "A figure of speech in which a word or phrase that designates one thing is applied to another in an implicit comparison."

(Fromkin 2003:204): "an expression that ordinarily designates one concept – its literal meaning – but is used to designate another concept."

(Fromkin 2003:584): "The essence of metaphor is understanding and experiencing one kind of thing in terms of another."

(Lakoff & Johnson 1980:5): "The essence of metaphor is understanding and experiencing one kind of thing in terms of another."

(Wright 2002:7-9): "Metaphors exist in all languages. . . A metaphor uses one idea to stand for another idea."

Idiom

American Heritage Dictionary (AHD 2000): "A speech form or an expression of a given language that is peculiar to itself grammatically or cannot be understood from the individual meanings of its elements."

(Ammer 1997:Preface): "a set phrase of two or more words that means something different from the literal meaning of the individual words . . . the true test of an idiom is whether it changes meaning when rendered word for word in another language."

(Fromkin 2003:584): "An expression whose meaning . . . may be unrelated to the meaning of its parts."

(Fromkin 2003:206): "they tend to be frozen in form and do not readily enter into other combinations or allow the word order to change."

(Spears 2005:v): Idioms are phrases that are "opaque or unpredictable because they don't have expected, literal meaning."

(Wright 2002:7-9): "an expression with the following features: 1. It is fixed and is recognized by native speakers. You cannot make up your own! 2. It uses language in a non-literal – metaphorical – way."

"Why are idioms and metaphors so important?"

(Wright 2002:9)

1. ". . . they are very common. It is impossible to speak, read, or listen to English without meeting idiomatic language. This is not something you can leave until you reach an advanced level. All native speaker English is idiomatic."

2. ". . . very often the metaphorical use of a word is more common than its literal use. . . . Often the literal meaning creates a picture in your mind, and this picture makes the other meanings easier to understand."

3. ". . . because it is fun to learn and to use. . . . if the language you are learning is more colourful and interesting, there is more chance that you will remember it. You will also sound more natural if your English contains more idioms."

Pragmatics

Pragmatics is about developing the metacognitive skill of understanding the full impact of one's linguistic creation upon others. For example, if, while talking to another person, a speaker says, "I don't believe him," and gives the listener neither a clue about whom the "him" refers to, nor any idea of what the "believing" refers to, then the listener is completely left in the dark about what the speaker is talking about. Moreover, if the speaker starts a monologue with this statement, never clarifies the antecedent of "him," and continues in this vein, the listener will become further and further lost as the monologue unfolds.

A good use of pragmatics will help the speaker learn how to choose words and present context from the point of view of the listener. Taking into consideration the knowledge and information the listener may or may not have about the topic being discussed is a

> **Pragmatics:** That part of semantics dealing with awareness of the linguistic as well as the situational context of what one says or writes.
> **Deixis:** A specific aspect of pragmatics that deals with awareness of the *who*, the *when* and the *where* of all utterances.

linguistic/social skill that will greatly enhance a speaker's performance. A major part of mastery of English or of any language is one's awareness of what a listener brings to the conversation.

As teachers, we must constantly hone this skill in the classroom, whether it is for children, teenagers, adults from the USA or adults from around the world. Just as we teachers must be models for this, so, in turn, it is incumbent upon us to build the same skill within the minds of our students. As a student begins to develop skill in pragmatics, his or her confidence will grow toward mastery of English. Linguistic skill, cultural/social skill and self-esteem all evolve hand in hand with this development.

Deixis is a specific aspect of pragmatics demonstrating awareness that expressions such as *now, last week* and *next spring* all imply a specific frame of time, that expressions such as *ours, this woman's belongings* and *those people* can only make sense when the context is clear to all listeners, and that expressions such as *here, over there* and *beyond that hill* can have meaning only when the relative location of the speaker is known to all involved in the discussion.

Test Your Knowledge (Exercise 13)
"The meaning of auxiliary verbs"

How will you explain the meaning of auxiliary verbs? If you explain that they are "helping verbs," and an EL states that in his or her language they don't have, nor do they need, such "helping verbs," what are you going to tell them? In exactly what way do they help us to understand the meaning of the verb?"

♦ In the phrase *have been studying* what is the main verb?

♦ What is the function and real meaning of *have?*

♦ What is the function and real meaning of *been?*

♦ Exactly how do these two auxiliary verbs help an EL to understand the nature of the action that is taking place in such a sentence?

Test Your Knowledge (Exercise 14)
"The meaning of modal auxiliary verbs"

Once your ELs have mastered the regular auxiliary verbs, their next step is to move on to the **Modal Auxiliary Verbs**. These words and phrases introduce a whole new dimension of confusion because they are in the subjunctive mood (hence, the word **modal**). Students must be able to comprehend words such as *can, could, shall, should, will, would, must, may, might,* and even such idiom modals as *be able to, be going to, ought to, have to, have got to, be supposed to, be about to, be to, be allowed to, be permitted to* and *used to.* These last phrases are idioms in that their internal grammar is not normal, and they need to be viewed as single constituents. They function as modal auxiliary verbs.

What is the real meaning of *would* in the expression: *would have been studying*? Most ELs are not accustomed to such words in their mother tongues, in which these meanings are often expressed by adverbs. In this exercise provide a range of definitions for *would* in ways that will be understandable to ELs:

The more that you are willing to explore such misunderstandings in the minds of your ELs, to listen to the details of their confusion and to apply extreme patience in explaining these seemingly unexplainable aspects of English grammar, the better ESL teacher you will become. It is very easy for us native speakers of English to go over these auxiliaries and other murky aspects of our grammar far too quickly. Part of the reason that we may want to hurry through this process is that we, ourselves, cannot explain this material with precise clarity. Our internal attitude may be, "Just shut up and learn it, so that I don't have to explain it." That can easily translate into quiet acceptance on the part of students and a continuation of their almost complete lack of understanding. That is not good enough for high quality ESL teaching.

We must "find" our students in this difficult process. It is our job as good ESL teachers to discover that "cutting edge" in their minds and build on that so that they themselves can generate further knowledge in each aspect of English grammar from what they know already.

While semantics is probably the most familiar aspect of linguistics to most speakers of English, we tend to take it for granted and to gloss over it lightly. By incorporating the concepts presented in this chapter, by entering an EL's grammatical frame of reference in your classroom and by listening carefully and understanding the confusion they experience in understanding the meaning of English sentences, teachers can help students develop methods of creating chain reactions of vocabulary building both for the classroom and throughout their lives.

Chapter 5

Phonemes: The Atoms of Language[1]

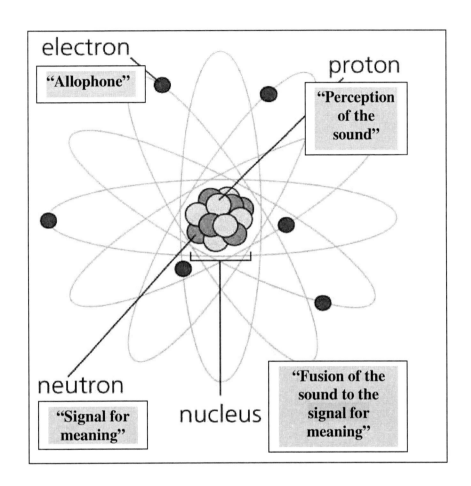

Phonology

The sound system of a language is usually ignored in the study of its grammar. This is why teachers need to acquire a good foundation in this crucial aspect of linguistics. It is the area where ESL adults have the most difficulty. They may be able to understand the grammar of English very well, translate well (especially back into their mother tongues) and even write English quite well, but invariably they fall short when it comes to the pronunciation of English sounds. Something very subjective and almost elusive is going on in the production of the sounds of a

---

[1] In the 1980s I used this phrase in courses I taught at UCLA for the purpose described in this chapter. Later I came across Mark Baker's book, *The Atoms of Language* (2001). However, our uses of this metaphor are in completely different areas of language study.

88

language outside one's mother tongue that teachers must become aware of in order to help non-native learners of English move toward fluency.

> **Phonology:** the broad study of the sounds of languages. It includes:
> **Phonemics:** the study of the "deep structure" of the sound system. This is the world of the perception of the crucial sounds of a given language.
> **Phonetics:** This concerns what we actually do with these perceptions, how we physically produce the sounds that we have internalized as natives of a given language.

This field is reserved for the last part of the book so that readers can use the grammatical foundation they are more familiar with (morphology, syntax and semantics) to develop an understanding of **phonology** [Greek: "the study of sounds"]. **Phonemics** is presented before **phonetics** (next chapter) in this book because it forms the basis from which phonetic results are created.

Some linguists may object to this, but excluding **phonetics** from **phonology** is absurd. We can view this field in another tree diagram:

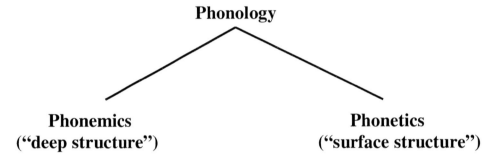

Phonology

Phonemics
("deep structure")

Phonetics
("surface structure")

Phonemes and Allophones

One can produce the accurate sounds of any language only if one has control of the complicated world of its **phonemes** and **allophones**.

Like atoms, the most fundamental building blocks of all matter, **phonemes** are the basis for everything that happens in language. A speaker's perception, understanding and creation of morphemes, words, constituents and sentences can happen only by expansion from these fundamental units. As we saw in Chapter 4 on semantics, the more one explores the "after shocks" of metaphors (the "semantic earthquakes" of language), the richer and more meaningful they become.

The cohesive force in the relationship between the proton and the neutron of an atom is reflected in the fusion of sound and the basis of meaning at the core of the phoneme. Phonemes do not carry full meaning themselves, but they "signal" meaning; that is, they are the originators, the most fundamental source of this union between sound and meaning. When the sound and the signal for meaning are "fused" together, the importance of this for language is reflected in the "strong nuclear force" that ties protons and neutrons together.

The "electrons" of phonemes are its **allophones**. Just as electrons travel in varying orbits around the nucleus of an atom, so we speakers of English are usually not consciously aware of the "location" of a phoneme's allophones. Sometimes they are far removed from our perception of them. Such is the case in *situation* [sɪčueš̌ən]. The /t/ goes far afield from what we perceive it to be. In this case, speakers of English are heavily influenced by the writing system. Though the allophones for /t/ in this word ([č] and [š]) are real sounds (unlike the phonemes they represent), they are somewhat "rebellious" toward the nucleus of the phoneme as they fly around it "in orbit."

Let's take a look at the phoneme /t/, whose phonetic result is a *voiceless alveolar stop,* to see how this works.

In the following diagram, the main sound [t] stands for what native speakers of English "hear" as a distinctive sound, unlike any other in the language. That is the purpose of showing a thick wall around this whole story of /t/[2] (see p. 88). Thus *cat* and *cap* are not the same concepts in English. The [t] of *cat* occupies a position of its own in the language such that it is capable of signaling a distinction in meaning from *cap*. No other sound in English can take the place of the [t]. [t] is given full individual authority to unite with [k] and [æ] in this particular order to make up this word.

> **Phoneme**: a learned, abstract perception of an individual **sound** in language that signals difference in **meaning** for a particular language. It sets up boundaries in order to contrast itself with the other distinctive sounds of that language. As such, it actually consists of a range of sounds (several different allophones) that comprise this subjective perception by a native speaker.
>
> **Allophones**: variations of sound that stand for a given phoneme. They are real sounds. Phonemes are **perceptions of sound**, not real sounds.

Two aspects of this word are required in order for the meaning to emerge for spoken English: 1. Only these three phonemes, represented phonetically as [k-æ-t], can work together for this concept, and 2. These three phonemes must occur in this particular order.

---

[2] Remember that brackets [t] stand for the actual sound (the allophone) of this phoneme, and slanted lines /t/ stand for the phoneme itself. The phoneme is a larger concept than the allophone since it includes all of the allophones belonging to that phoneme. The allophone is the actual phonetic result coming out of a speaker's mouth.

Though it is a world of its own, the reality of /t/ is that we native speakers of English "tolerate" other sounds to stand for /t/ even when they are not this sound at all. They can even be far removed from the actual sound of [t], and yet we "hear" them as /t/s. These variations are the **allophones** of the phoneme /t/. The Greek source for this word is helpful in understanding it: "other sounds" for the sound of /t/.

In this diagram the other sounds are some of this phoneme's allophones [tʰ, ʔ, č, š and ɾ]. All together, in this view, there are six actual sounds for /t/, the five just mentioned and the [t] itself.

The Phoneme /t/ and Six of its Allophones:

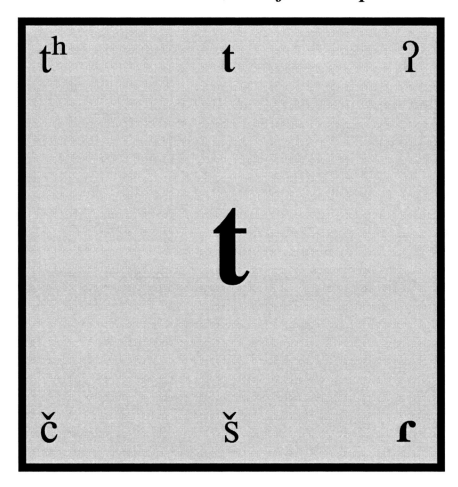

[t]   as in *start* [stɑrt] or *loft* [lɔft]
This is the "true" [t]. In general, it shows up reliably at the ends of words.

[tʰ]   as in *told* [told]
Most of the time in American English this phoneme is aspirated at the beginning of words when a vowel follows immediately.

[ʔ]   as in *button* [bʌʔən] (refer to the story of Alvin Allophone below)
Our mouths are lazy. It is easier to put this glottal stop between vowels than it is to produce a real [t] in that position.

[č]   as in *situation* [sɪčuešən]
With this allophone there really is a [t], but it occurs only at the beginning of the sound. In reality this sound is a consonant cluster, but we do not perceive it that way. It is a *voiceless palatal affricate*.

[š]   This is the second allophone for /t/ in *situation* [sɪčuešən].
It is a *voiceless palatal fricative* [š]; it sounds like the *sh* in *ship*.

[ɾ]   as in *little* [lɪɾəl]
This is called a "flap;" it is actually a "baby [d]." Again our mouths are lazy. It is easier to continue voicing the alveolar stop between two voiced sounds than it is to devoice it as we normally do when making a [t].

Of the six allophones shown within the box for /t/ above, three are English phonemes /t, č and s/, while the other three [tʰ, ʔ and ɾ] are "only allophones," not phonemes.

Why is this the case? It has to do with the way speakers of English perceive the sounds, not how the sounds are made objectively. A spectrograph reading would show that all six are, indeed, different sounds, made in different parts of the mouth, but speakers of English ignore these differences and "hear" all six sounds as the letter *T*. In order to gain mastery of English (including the writing system), they must insert the letter *T* in all the proper places regardless of the way this phoneme and all of its variations are pronounced objectively.

As a result, English speakers ignore aspiration [tʰ], the glottal stop[ʔ] and the flap [ɾ] and simply consider them all to be *T*s. They are of a "lower status" in the phonemic system of English (like Alvin Allophone and his "plight" in the story below) and are passed over for consideration as phonemes. This is an entirely subjective choice on the part of English speakers. This does not make English inferior (all languages do this), but it is a reality which ELs must comprehend. The [č] and the [š] are two other phonemes which are "stolen" temporarily for use as the *T*.

The American English[3] Phonemic Chip

The contrastive distance between each of the 40 phonemes in American English is crucial in the formation of morphemes and words. Apart from a few single-phoneme words and morphemes, such as *Oh* and *–s,* full meaning is created only when a string of phonemes, uttered in a particular sequence, is produced by a speaker of English. When one says *cat* (and not *tack*), it is only this very combination of these three distinct phonemes in this particular order which can receive the full meaning of a "feline animal." This combination occurs in a paradox. This union of sound and meaning can only occur when each phoneme is, on the one hand, independent and is perceived as unlike any other sound of the language, and, on the other, when it becomes subsequently united (dependent) with other phonemes in a string of sounds to make a word.

This organization of sounds creates an infinite set of combination possibilities as long as these combinations are acceptable to the ears of English speakers. "Unused" combinations of this sort are **lexical gaps** such as those created by Lewis Carroll and Dr. Seuss (see Chapter 2 for more on lexical gaps).

As very young children we quickly **acquire** the distinctive sounds of our mother tongue. It doesn't matter which language our mother tongue is; it has a distinct set of phonemes that will organize our perception and production of language sounds for the rest of our lives. These phonemes flood into our **LAD's (language acquisition devices).**[4]

---

[3] The phrase "American English" refers to what is called "General American English" (GAE) or "Standard American English" (SAE). This is sometimes called the "Pennsylvania Dialect" since that is the region from which it originated early in American history.

[4] This concept was originated by Noam Chomsky, and it refers to the innate abilities of all humans to acquire, develop and eventually speak a language. One can think of them as "linguistic templates" waiting to be filled by the adults who surround the child. Chomsky would assert that these templates are already rather sophisticated when we are born, capable of incorporating specific linguistic data from a given language, almost a process of "filling in the blanks" of an innate language structure in the brain.

Once they are well established in the brains of children, the analogy of a computer chip for these phonemes comes to mind. Just as the central processing unit (CPU) is the most fundamental operating device for a computer, so the "Phonemic Chip" becomes the originator of all that happens in our later development of language. We native speakers of English could put a sign on our foreheads stating **"English Phonemes Inside."**

By the age of seven, most children who grow up with native speakers of American English have acquired the forty phonemes shown in the "chip" below. This CPU for the sound system of English determines the way children perceive these distinct sounds of the language and the way they manipulate their mouths to produce them. Once they are produced, they are no longer phonemes; they are now phonetic representations of the phonemes buried deeply in this "brain chip." None of the 40 are "pure sounds." All of them have a degree (in some cases a high degree) of subjectivity attached to them.

Each box contains a phoneme. As with the /t/ described above, each phoneme has a number of allophones that would be contained within each box. The thick walls between the phonemes are important. They indicate the all-important boundaries between phonemes, their very reason for existence. The whole range of sounds (the main phoneme and all its allophones) within each box is heard and interpreted by native speakers of English as one sound, that is, one phoneme, even though the differences in sounds (the allophones) are provable by a spectrograph.

The 40th phoneme of Standard American English (bottom right) is still used by older people, but it is disappearing from the language. For them *witch* and *which* are pronounced differently with a "hw" sound at the beginning of *which* [ʍɪč] For the majority of speakers of SAE these two words are pronounced exactly the same; thus, for them there are only 39 phonemes.

In this "chip" we are simply picking on /t/. It happens to have many variations of sound (allophones). Many of the other phonemes in the chart also have allophones: the Schwa is an allophone for many of the other vowels, and /p/ includes an aspirated version [pʰ] as does /k/: [kʰ].

The American English Phonemic Chip

(The forty phonemes: only /t/ is shown with its allophones;
most of the other phonemes also have allophones.)

a	æ	ai	au	b
č	d	e	ɛ	ə
f	g	h	i	ɪ
j	k	l	m	n
ŋ	o	ɔ	oi	p
r	s	š	tʰ t ʔ t č š ɾ	θ
ð	u	ʊ	ʌ	v
w	y	z	ž	ʍ

Alvin Allophone and the Trusty Allophonometer

Once upon a time a sad soul by the name of Alvin (a.k.a. Glottal Stop, Esq. and sometimes referred to as [ʔ]) was looking for a home in the Kingdom of Anglia. He was sad because the People of Anglia had never recognized him. His importance had been brutally ripped away, his very existence denied. So important was he, in fact, that words beginning with vowels at the start of a sentence or said in isolation begin with him, but nobody recognized this basic fact. He would point out that in order to say the word *apple,* in isolation, a speaker would not really begin with a vowel at all (vowels are sounds made in the mouth with no restriction).

"Quite the contrary," he would say, "Whenever *apple* (or almost any word beginning with a vowel) begins a sentence, in order to get to the sound of *a*, every speaker in Anglia has to make that all-important stop, completely at the bottom of the throat, at the very beginning of the sound in order to release the puff of air that produces the sound of *a*. In fact, I am so important that the People of Anglia should grant me full phonemic citizenship."

"Nonsense!" they would say. "You don't belong here; you are neither a vowel nor a consonant. In fact, you don't exist at all! You don't even have papers to show your citizenship in Anglia. How preposterous of you to request phonemehood! We have well established and utterly distinguished phonemes here in Anglia and have been doing quite well for centuries without you, thank you very much!"

Alvin said, "Well, if I can't be a full-fledged phoneme in Anglia, could I, at least, apply to be an allophone?"

"Where could you fit in?" the People asked. "We have a well-ordered House of Forty Phonemes, all distinguished Lords and Ladies they are! Each one has its well established and reliable set of allophones. Who needs you? What makes you think that, in your lowly status, you could possibly offer anything of use to even one of our distinguished phonemes?"

Alvin took things into his own hands and went to the castles of each of the fifteen Ladies of the Vowels to seek citizenship. He pointed out that he was always present at the very inception of any word beginning with a vowel and said in isolation. All of the Ladies were deeply offended by this impudent young man claiming to have importance above and beyond their very existence. "Get out of here, you despicable ragamuffin! Didn't someone say you are a bastard? We don't want the likes of you around here. If you show up here again, it will be 'Off with your head!'"

In a state of deep sadness, Alvin wandered the forest around Anglia, wondering if anybody would take him in, even as a lowly allophone when he knew full well that he should qualify as a full phoneme. After all, glottal stops have a life in many other languages outside of Anglia. *What is the matter with these people?*

It was raining cats and dogs in the forest as Alvin stumbled along, lonely, cold and hungry. Just as he was about to give up the ghost, he happened upon the castle of Lord Trevor The T, a highly respected Lord of the Consonants and a distinguished phoneme in Anglia. A short distance from the castle a funny little happy man was dancing in the rain next to his garden and singing:

> *With a little bit of luck*
> *With a little bit of luck*
> *With a little bit*
> *Of bloomin' luck.*

Immediately Alvin knew that he was actually pronouncing the words this way: [wɪθ ʔə lɪʔəl bɪʔ]. He knew that every time the man sang *a little bit,* he was actually singing the real sound that was Alvin's *raison d'être.* All of those ʔ's were glottal stops, but the people of Anglia thought they were /t/s or vowel sounds at the beginning of words. They were actually made at the opposite end of the mouth, but the people "heard" most of them as /t/s.

After his song Alvin came up to him, all wet and drippy, but with a faint smile on his face. "Good afternoon, Sir," he said, "What a lovely song! Where did you learn that?"

"Well, son," the man said, "my name is Doolittle (he actually pronounced it as [dulɪʔəl]). Didn't you see the movie *My Fair Lady*? I am Eliza Doolittle's father."

Alvin sighed. "Mine, Sir, is a sad story" he said. "I have never seen a movie, for I am very poor."

"Cheer up, my son," said Mr. Doolittle. "After I became famous in that story, the people of London threw me out because they said I talked funny. So, I left, wandered around in the countryside for a long time and eventually came upon this forest where I became the gardener for Lord Trevor The T. My life is not so bad, and as for you, my son, *With a little bit of luck you'll be OK.*"

"Oh, Mr. Doolittle, could you get me an appointment with Lord Trevor The T?" said Alvin anxiously, "I have something very important to ask him."

"*With a little bit of luck,*" said Doolittle, "I probably could."

"Oh, thank you, Kind Sir!"

Doolittle arranged for a meeting between Alvin and Lord Trevor The T in his castle. On his way in Alvin remarked, "Look how thick those walls are!"

Upon meeting Lord Trevor in his royal chamber, Alvin bowed obsequiously and said, "Your Eminence, thank you for allowing me to discuss my concern with you. I am a Glottal Stop, and, as I am sure you know, we Glottal Stops are considered to be very important in many languages outside of Anglia, but there seems to be no recognition of my very existence here. In some languages my sound is so important that it is even considered a phoneme. I know that would not be possible here in Anglia, but with your permission I would like to be considered an allophone in your royal house. I would love to be on your phonemic team. Is there any possibility for such consideration?"

"Well, my son," said Lord Trevor, "you have been very polite in your request. As you know, we already have our well established allophones such as [tʰ], the flap [ɾ], [č] and [š], but if you can prove that you are, indeed, an allophone of /t/, I will consider your request, but you must make a convincing case."

"Oh, thank you, My Lord. I would like to request the presence of Lord Alphonse, Chancellor of the Anglian Allophones, with his trusty Allophonometer here at the court to demonstrate the truth of my claim. Let him and the people of your court decide if my request is legitimate."

Lord Trevor said, "Excellent, my son, let the people of my court along with the high services of Lord Alphonse settle this matter once and for all. I will request the presence of Lord Alphonse immediately."

Within a fortnight Lord Alphonse with his Allophonometer and his retinue of loyal servants arrived at the Castle of Lord Trevor with great fanfare. Lord Alphonse placed his Allophonometer on an ornate table in the middle of the court and said to Alvin, "Proceed, Master Alvin, with your allophonic request."

Alvin said, "Please allow me to present Mr. Doolittle and his song. If you would be so kind as to turn on your Allophonometer while Mr. Doolittle sings his song, we can see if he produces any Glottal Stops while he sings."

Mr. Doolittle sang his song and when he got to the chorus:

With a little bit of luck
With a little bit of luck
With a little bit
You can't go wrong,

the Allophonometer registered a total of seven glottal stops where the written text showed the letter T and three more at the beginning of the word *a*.

Alvin said, "Your Eminence, Lord Trevor The T, do you see how many glottal stops there are in this chorus alone?"

"Good Gracious Me," said Lord Trevor, "I had no idea there could be so many glottal stops in such a short amount of text."

"But wait a minute!" the People said, "Why are you listening to Mr. Doolittle? He told us himself that he was kicked out of London because he doesn't speak correctly. How could you listen to him? And, furthermore, he's a ragamuffin. Look, he can't [kænʔ] even button [bʌʔən] up his own shirt!"

"Would you kindly repeat your last sentence," said Alvin.

"We said he can't [kænʔ] even button [bʌʔən] up his own shirt!"

Alvin turned to Lord Alphonse to see the results of this dialogue. "Lord Alphonse, what is the reading from your Allophonometer? The words they used are spelled c-a-n-'-t and b-u-t-t-o-n, but how are they actually pronounced?"

Lord Alphonse said, "Well, I do declare, the Allophonometer tells us that they pronounced these words with glottal stops, not actual Ts."

"What?" said the People, "That can't be! *Button* is spelled with two T's. How could anyone say that they were not T's?"

Lord Alphonse turned to Lord Trevor The T and said, "Your Highness, before Alvin came here, no one in Anglia even bothered to investigate whether or not the glottal stop was used as an allophone to any phoneme. By Jove, I think Alvin is right after all."

"Let the people say that last sentence one more time just to make sure," said Alvin.

So the people again said, "He can't [kænʔ] even button [bʌʔən] up his own shirt!"

Lord Alphonse said, "There you have it. There can be no doubt. My trusty Allophonometer has registered that glottal stop every time they say those two words. So, I think that there is, indeed, a place for Alvin among your allophones, Lord Trevor."

There was great celebration at the court. Alvin was given full citizenship and the glorious name of Alvin Allophone, trusted and loyal servant of His Eminence, Lord Trevor The T.

Alvin Allophone had finally found his proper place in the House of the English Phonemes and lived happily ever after in the majestic Castle of Lord Trevor The T.

The End

[Source: Original]

Phonemic Awareness

Phonemic awareness (PA) is crucial for any member of a literate society who hopes to participate fully in its social institutions.

Millions of adult Americans do not have, nor ever will have, full phonemic awareness. One of the main purposes of a book and course such as this is "not to cry over spilt milk," but to pick up the pieces and create leverage in the efficient use of linguistic skills so that we can begin to rise quickly to a level of literacy that befits a modern, highly industrialized nation such as the USA.

What is phonemic awareness? Full **phonemic awareness** consists of the complete and accurate coordination of all aspects of the sound system of a given language along with the representation of those sounds by the writing system. This full coordination allows the speaker to be able to:

   I. Hear the speech sounds of others, accurately placing each sound in the "phonemic chip" of that language,
  II. Produce the full range of sounds (the phonetic results) that represent those phonemes (the main phoneme and all of its allophones); that is, to speak in such a way that a listener can easily do step #1,
 III. Decipher the phonemes as symbolized in the writing system,
 IV. Accurately read such writing; that is, to recognize all the phonemes and allophones represented in the writing and then to reproduce such writing either silently or aloud, and
  V. Write English with the full range of phonemes, accurately representing all the allophones and their possible variant spellings for any given phoneme.

This is an astonishingly complex process, especially in the case of English, and that is because there is no reliable connection between the writing and the sounds of English. We are stuck with the writing of English as it was spoken 600 years ago. It is no wonder that many natives of American English never achieve full phonemic awareness.

The Race Toward Phonemic Awareness

A. The Reliable Process
Matching up the phonemes with those symbols of the English alphabet which consistently stand for the actual sound: **/b, d, f, h, j, k, l, m, n, p, r, s, t, v, w, z/**. Here the early learner can see that there is a fairly reliable and predictable relationship between the symbol and the sound. This becomes the basis for moving into the murky territory of Step B.

B. The Unreliable Process: Phonics
Here the learner must (1) discover the **unreliable** but **crucial** relationships between writing patterns and their corresponding sounds; (2) learn to ignore "useless" letters such as **c, q** and **x;** and (3) develop extreme flexibility with the sounds of the "5 vowels:" **a, e, i, o, u.** In reality, there are 15 vowels: 3 prominent diphthongs, 3 lesser ones and 9 relatively "pure" vowels. Example of the unreliability: English writing displays at least 40 different spellings of the Schwa [ə] alone (see the next chapter and inside the back cover).

C. Fixing the 40 Phonemes of English
Capitalizing on the flexibility already developed, the learner must now "complete the picture" of the full sound system of English. The crucial aspect of this step is coupling the 40 sounds with the knowledge that there are essential "walls" between any two of these sounds. Each sound, each phoneme, must be clearly perceived as that sound alone and not any other.

D. Learning All of the Allophones
To gain control of the sound system as it unites with the writing system, the learner must now accept and recognize in written English all of the variations of actual sounds that belong with a given phoneme (i.e., its allophones). For example, for the phoneme **/t/**, the learner must be able to "hear" that [t, tʰ, ʔ, ɾ, č, š] all stand for **/t/** in specific situations and are perceived by English speakers to be that letter alone in contrast to all of the other 39 phonemes.

Why is it a Race to Phonemic Awareness?

The English we write today is not far removed from William Caxton's introduction of printing in 1475. If our writing system had been introduced recently, then there would be little separation between the writing and the sound system, and this whole issue of phonemic awareness would not be so complicated and urgent.

Turkish is an example of a writing system introduced within the last century; as a result, phonemic awareness emerges easily with young learners because the relationship between the sound and the letters is transparent and consistent. On the other hand, most highly educated Turks are unable to read any of their literature written before 1928. That is the year when Mustafa Kemal Atatürk single-handedly removed the Turkish language from its Ottoman past. For nearly 700 years Turks wrote in the Arabic script; this was Ottoman, essentially the same language as Turkish. In order to modernize his country, Atatürk turned his society directly toward Europe, forcing the use of the Roman letters. There are photographs of him going around Istanbul with chalk and easel teaching the new letters. The result is a very streamlined and efficient language. However, the Turks are cut off from their literary past.

Like it or not, we are stuck with the complicated and maddeningly inconsistent spelling of English. With all of its problems, speakers and writers of English are so deeply invested in this vast literary movement that there is no turning back, no possibility of avoiding the difficult process of pairing up the sound system with the writing system. The two are deeply separated, and every learner has no choice but to find his or her way through the murkiness, and she or he must do so in a hurry.

There is, indeed, a sense of urgency concerning PA. The early years are crucial in the development of PA. If a child does not have age-appropriate PA by the end of 4th grade, it is getting late, and unless remedial steps are taken, such a child will fall further behind each successive year. Catching up becomes harder and harder. We teachers must rush our children through the process of PA even before their minds are mature enough to comprehend the complexity of what they are learning. At an almost premature age, we must help them to become "airborne" in the learning of English before their time. They need to acquire the **metacognitive** skills of learning more about their language by the use of what they know already. This can only happen if they are phonemically aware as young children.

Another way to view the process depicted above is to facilitate and monitor a learner's journey through the following steps:

Step I: <u>Hearing and Internalizing the Phonemes</u>

The 26 letters of the English alphabet do reflect (sometimes, unfortunately, very dimly) the phonemes of the language, and 16 of the letters for consonants are generally quite good at representing those sounds.[5] It is important for young learners to be able to grasp this consistent foundation for the relationship between sound and letter. They must build on this foundation. We suggest that teachers dwell on these 16 consonants first when writing is introduced to young learners. In order to do so, naturally you will have to use vowels, but rather than giving children the immense confusion of vowels at the beginning, they should appear in words rather inconspicuously. The most powerful way to teach these 16 symbols for 16 of the English phonemes **/b, d, f, h, j, k, l, m, n, p, r, s, t, v, w, z/** is by the use of **minimal pairs** and **minimal sets**.

> **Minimal pairs:** These are two words which are exactly the same except for one phoneme. That one phoneme is enough to make them have different meaning. Examples with 3 different locations of the different phoneme within the word: 1. (initially) *bat – rat,* 2. (medially) *bad – bed,* 3. (finally) *bat – bad.* Minimal pairs are a powerful tool to learn and reinforce the phonemic system of any language. Learners must be able to hear and perceive the difference in sound as it relates to difference in meaning.
>
> **Minimal sets**: These are simply more than two of the same pattern. It is useful for teachers to fill out minimal sets as much as is feasible for young learners. The more examples they see, the more strongly becomes their awareness of phonemic difference.

Words such as *cat* are impossible to avoid, but teachers must be aware of its pitfalls. The letter *c* really has no life in English. It is either a *k* or an *s,* and since those letters already exist, this confusion only tampers with the phonemic foundation being set at this early stage. Simply be aware of this and try to concentrate on the 16 letters given above:

---

[5] Of course, there are exceptions. Why, for example, is there a *w* in *answer,* a *b* in *debt,* an *l* in *could,* etc.? Only the history of these words can answer that. For the young learner, these are the relatively few exceptions that simply have to be learned. It is best to set them aside at the beginning.

Using Minimal Pairs and Sets to Teach
The 16 "Consistent" Consonants of American English
(Their forms as phonemes: /b, d, f, h, j, k, l, m, n, p, r, s, t, v, w, z/)

Teaching the initial phoneme **Teaching the medial phoneme** **Teaching the final phoneme**

Minimal Pairs

bat	more
hat	door
fire	seat
liar	heat
tame	boil
same	foil

bad	kicker
bed	kisser
food	reader
fad	reaper
easy	laser
eery	later

bat	more
bad	mode
fire	seat
fine	seed
lame	boil
late	boys

When you present these to students, watch yourself closely to make sure that there is only one different phoneme in the pair in precisely the same location and that you have exactly the same number of phonemes in each word of the pair. Beware that you don't allow combinations such as *bat – brat, bat – BART, fire – flyer, fire – choir,* etc. *Fire* has three phonemes, phonetically spelled [f-ai-r], and *choir* has four [k-w-ai-r]. Also notice that the number of phonemes in English often does not match the number of letters: *seat* has four letters but only three phonemes.

Minimal Sets

bat	more
hat	door
cat	lore
fat	four
rat	sore
sat	core
mat	boar
gnat	nor

It is difficult to produce minimal sets for this group. Simply expand on the pairs shown above.

bat	seat
bad	seed
ban	sear
bang	seam
bam	seize
bass	cease
batch	seal
badge	seek

Using Minimal Pairs and Sets to Teach
The 8 "Inconsistent" Consonants of American English[6]
(Their forms as phonemes: /č, g, ŋ, š, θ, ð, y, ž/)

| Teaching the
initial phoneme | Teaching the
medial phoneme | Teaching the
final phoneme |

Minimal Pairs

thin shin	yet Chet		teacher teaser	singer Caesar		wish win	swish swig
that chat	thick Shick		seizure Caesar	Mather matter		mash match	loath loathe
shop chop	those chose		ether either	wither wicker		ring reach	fling fleece

Minimal Sets

thin	yet			wish	sing
shin	Chet	It is difficult to		win	seat
fin	get	produce minimal		witch	seem
win	set	sets for this		with	seize
chin	let	group. Simply		wig	seethe
din	met	expand on the		wick	cease
yin	pet	pairs shown		wit	siege
bin	bet	above.		will	seal

Using Minimal Pairs and Sets to Teach
The 15 Vowels of American English
(Their forms as phonemes: /a, æ, ai, au, e, ɛ, ə, i, ɪ, o, ɔ, oi, u, ʊ, ʌ/)

Teaching the initial phoneme	Teaching the medial phoneme	Teaching the final phoneme[7]

Minimal Pairs

I've	awe	bit	miter	Sophie	psyche
of	Oh!	bat	meter	sofa	psycho
egg	oak	love	reader	Cody	marrow
Ugh!	eke	live	rider	coda	Mary
oil	even	sing	fling	Jello	Karo
eel	oven	sang	flung	jelly	carry

Minimal Sets

oil	even	bit	lead		
eel	oven	bat	lad		
all	Ivan	but	load		
ill	Evan	boot	lewd		
Al		boat	laud		
aisle		beat	lid		
ale		bought	loud		
owl		bet	lied		

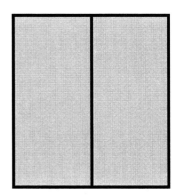

---

[7] Compared to many other languages, English tends to avoid words which end in vowels. They are found quite often in proper names, but finding minimal sets is probably not worth the effort.

Apply the same care when presenting minimal sets, but make them as long as you can for the students. The longer the set is, the more the phonemic patterns become internalized in the students' minds.

You cannot say what you cannot hear, and you cannot fully "hear" all of the phonemes of English until they are clear to you from the people who have control of the language.

Step II: <u>Speaking Accurately</u>

Now you must be able to reproduce in speech all the phonemes and their allophonic variations. It is best for students to focus on what they hear when you make your minimal pairs and sets. At first they should not be heavily influenced by the writing of the words shown.

Steps III & IV: <u>Deciphering the Written Language and Reading</u>

You cannot read what you have not heard and said. Full coordination of hearing and speaking is a prerequisite to effective reading. Naturally, at this stage, students must enter the murky world of English spelling. This is where phonemic awareness begins to get tricky. The learning of reading can only be effective if they have control of Steps I and II.

As a teacher, you must take your students carefully into the world of reading. It is easy for many students to become overwhelmed by the written word and begin to give up the drive toward mastery. This is where phonics becomes absolutely crucial, and the student needs to feel that she or he can manage the onslaught of English writing. The written word and all of the 40 phonemes learned must match up in the minds of students.

Just as the student will profit from relative consistency in the learning of the first 16 consonants, so it is important that the teacher spend considerable effort in having students feel grounded in those phonics patterns which are relatively consistent. That is the foundation upon which students can begin tentatively to explore bizarre spelling patterns such as *answer, debt, could, aisle, corps, knight* and all of those rascally *–ough* words: *rough, cough, bough, through, though, hiccough*, etc.

Step V: <u>Writing at Age-Appropriate Levels</u>

If you can read effectively in English, you are now ready to learn how to write it. Naturally, the English a student writes must reflect the reading he or she is able to do. This is where the rubber meets the road. Writing forces the student to make a commitment to the coordination of all of these five steps. This is where a student shows conclusively that all aspects of the linguistic system of English have been internalized and unified; she/he is now **phonemically aware**.

Remember that these five steps do not happen in strict sequence. All four need to be going on at the same time from the beginning, but a student can only move conclusively to the next step if the previous one is under control.

The race is to bring students effectively, and before it is too late, along a path that unites all of these elements in the student's mind. Only this can produce genuine literacy.

Test Your Knowledge (Exercise 15)
"Why don't we just dispense with phonemes?"

After all, haven't we already learned that phonemes are not real? No one can actually utter a phoneme; so, what is the point of learning about them? Explain in your own words why phonemes are not only important for everyone to learn, but are, in fact, the single most important concept that any learner of language must comprehend and internalize. No matter what their age, they simply cannot move forward in any language without phonemes. Why is this the case?

Test Your Knowledge (Exercise 16)
"What is the difference between allophones and phonemes?"

A. Which of these two is real in the sense that one can actually utter it, and exactly what does "real" mean?

B. Give an example of two words in English that show two different allophones of the phoneme /k/. How are they different? Why is it important for speakers of English to consider them to be the same?

Test Your Knowledge (Exercise 17)
"Minimal pairs"

A. What are we investigating in the pairs *vim* and *dim?* Why is this important for speakers of English?

B. Apply the same questions to *dim* and *doom:*

C. Apply the same questions to *doom* and *dupe:*

Chapter 6

Phonetics:
The Public Display of Phonemes

Phonemes constitute the "deep structure" of phonology. Once those phonemes are implanted in the minds of a speaker, they go through a very complicated process before they are released from the mouth. The phonological rules of a language govern that process. They "gather in" the allophones of a phoneme to make them acceptable for inclusion within the confines of a given phoneme; they manipulate these distinctive sounds to fit the phonological requirements of English; and they determine how those phonemes are to be released from the mouth. The speaker must then coordinate all of this information about an utterance from the brain to the vocal tract, and finally the utterance (the "surface structure") is released from the mouth:

> **Phonemics:** the identification of a native speaker's perception of the distinctive sounds of a language including all relevant allophones. This is the comprehensive study of the sound system in the minds of speakers, in their "phonemic chips."
> **Phonetics:** the study of what a native speaker does with those "mind sounds" to produce a result in the mouth. It investigates the mechanical processes at work in the vocal tract along with the way those sounds are represented in writing.

Phonetics ("Surface Structure")

Motor nerve coordination with the vocal tract

Phonological Rules

↑

Phonemics ("Deep Structure")

This chapter concerns the surface structure of sounds as they are produced in the vocal tract, passed through the air and then received by the ear of the listener. This is the public display of those crucial sounds, the phonemes. It has to fit the linguistic expectations of the person speaking and anyone listening to an utterance in English. They have to agree in a general sense although there is an amazing amount of variation among the 350 million native speakers of English in the way that they perceive and understand this process. As a result, each utterance and the understanding thereof is, in many cases, almost a miracle since no two people have exactly the same phonological understanding of their native tongues.

Nevertheless, there is enough agreement between speaker and listener that successful communication does take place most of the time. When a speaker of English wants to express a thought concerning a *root*, he or she will take the three phonemes embedded in the mental chip /r-u-t/[1] and do whatever is necessary according to the phonological rules of English to produce the phonetic result: [r-u-t][2]. At first glance, this may appear to be ridiculously simple; aren't all of these sounds the same? What could possibly be tricky about going from the phonemes /r-u-t/ to the phonetic results [r-u-t]?

In the first place, speakers of American English have a particular way in which they pronounce [r]. It involves a retroflex type of action with the tip of the tongue which is not common among most of the world's languages. Since the speaker and the listener both know this pattern, they don't need to belabor the way they pronounce it or hear it.

However, a speaker of Spanish will have a very different set of rules to apply to the pronunciation of [r], and a speaker of French will produce this consonant at the opposite end of the vocal tract such that is it not the same sound at all. And, the speaker of Japanese will hear this sound in such a way that it sounds to him or her as if it might even be an [l].

Now, our speaker of English may want to express a thought with the word *loot,* and the listener and all other speakers of English will agree wholeheartedly that *loot* and *root* are not the same thing at all. We natives of English might even say, "How could anyone confuse these two words? They are completely different. What is the matter with them that they don't hear the difference?"

The only way that this distinction can be so obvious to speakers of English is because /l/ and /r/ are two completely different phonemes allied to a completely different set of expectations as to meaning. To the speaker of Japanese these are simply two different allophones of one phoneme. Japanese children learned very

---

[1] Phonemic symbols are enclosed in forward slashes / _ /.
[2] Phonetic symbols are enclosed in brackets [_]. Notice that these symbols appear to be the same as the symbols for the phonemes. Bear in mind, however, that /r-u-t/ is a much larger concept than [r-u-t], which is a simplified version of the phonetic result produced by the mouth. /r-u-t/ incorporates all of the possible allophones for these three phonemes. [r-u-t] stands for real sounds while /r-u-t/ stands for the abstract perceptions of these sounds.

early in their lives from their parents that the thick phonemic walls between /l/ and /r/, in the case of English, simply do not exist in Japanese. These two sounds should be "heard" simply as two variations (allophones) of one phoneme.

Therefore, while the distinction between *loot* and *root* is totally clear to speakers of English, that is not the case for speakers of Japanese. This demonstrates that the process of going from a phoneme to a phonetic result is, in fact, very subjective and is bound to the phonological expectations of a given language.

Back to our original word *root*. The speaker wants to express a complete thought about the root system of some plant and chooses these three phonemes in this order [r-u-t] to express this concept. Then, he or she makes all necessary adjustments to the perception of these phonemes and releases a result from his or her mouth in such a way that the English speaking listener takes this string of sounds passing through the air into his or her ears and processes the word in the reverse. If the listener understands the word, then the communication has been successful.

What did the speaker have to do to release those three phonemes in a phonetically successful manner? The remainder of this chapter is devoted to an explanation of this process.

Consonants vs. Vowels

Consonants: sounds made in the mouth with some type of restriction to the flow of air. The range of restriction goes from stops to liquids and glides. These last 2 are almost "vowels" because the restriction is so slight. Consonants are either voiced or voiceless.

Vowels: sounds made in the mouth with no restriction of the airflow. All of them are voiced. In the case of English, some are "pure" sounds, some are "lesser diphthongs," and a few are prominent diphthongs.

Let's begin with the difference between consonants and vowels. In the case of English all sounds are made by the outflow of air from the lungs either through the mouth or through the nose.[3] That is, they are all **egressive.** When air goes through the mouth, sounds are made by the configurations made primarily by the tongue with other parts of the mouth.

All **vowels** are **voiced**; that is, their sounds are made while the **vocal cords** are vibrating. They are made with **no restriction** to the flow of air as it goes through the mouth.

---

[3] Some languages such as the "click" languages of southern Africa use **ingressive** sounds. That is, air is taken into the mouth to produce the sound.

Some **consonants** are voiced, while others are **voiceless** (or "unvoiced"). Voiceless sounds are made without vibration of the vocal cords, as if one were whispering. The crucial difference with vowels is that consonants are made with **some type of restriction** given to the air flowing through the mouth or nose.

It will be helpful if you become familiar with the following two depictions of the human vocal tract. By referring your students to them often, you will help them to objectify the physical process of making the sounds of language. The more they can visualize their vocal tracts (like a cross section viewed from the side), the better they will be able to manipulate their mouths to form the correct pronunciations of the 40 phonemes of English.

As an ESL/EFL teacher it is important to remember that your teaching is not for yourself or for other native speakers of English. Though this may appear obvious, one of the mistakes we can make is to speak too quickly and without enough articulation for our students to hear the sounds distinctly. We must slow down and slightly "exaggerate" the distinct sounds of each word. This may feel a bit artificial at first, but, especially with the relative overuse of intonation in English, many of the sounds may not come through clearly to ELs. Paying close attention to exactly what your students can actually perceive will raise the quality of your teaching significantly.

As you do this, be sure that you don't change the pronunciation of the words you articulate. For example, a common mistake is to alter the sound of *a* in the phrase *a book* so that it becomes [e bʊk], rather than the real pronunciation [əbʊk].

The Human Vocal Tract

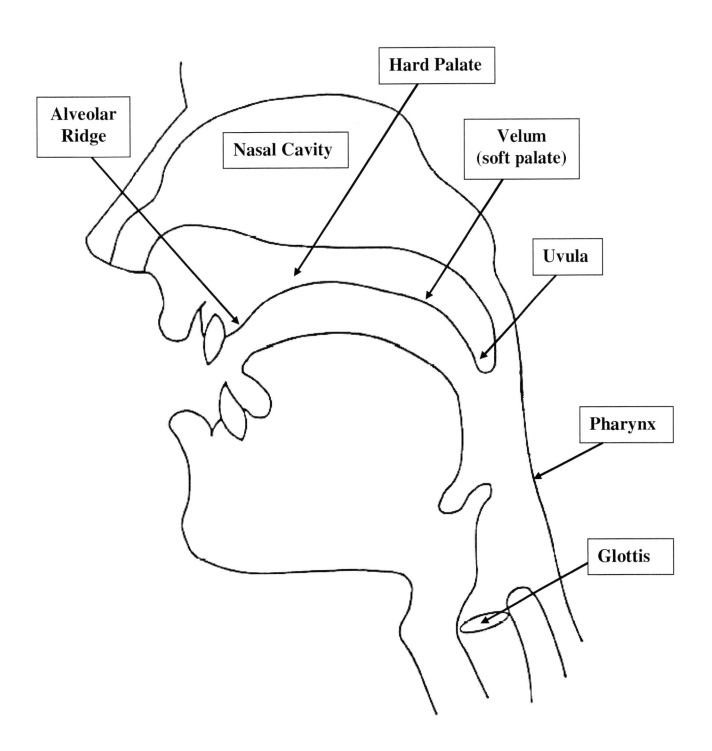

Hard Palate

Alveolar Ridge

Nasal Cavity

Velum (soft palate)

Uvula

Pharynx

Glottis

The Human Vocal Tract
(Places of Articulation)

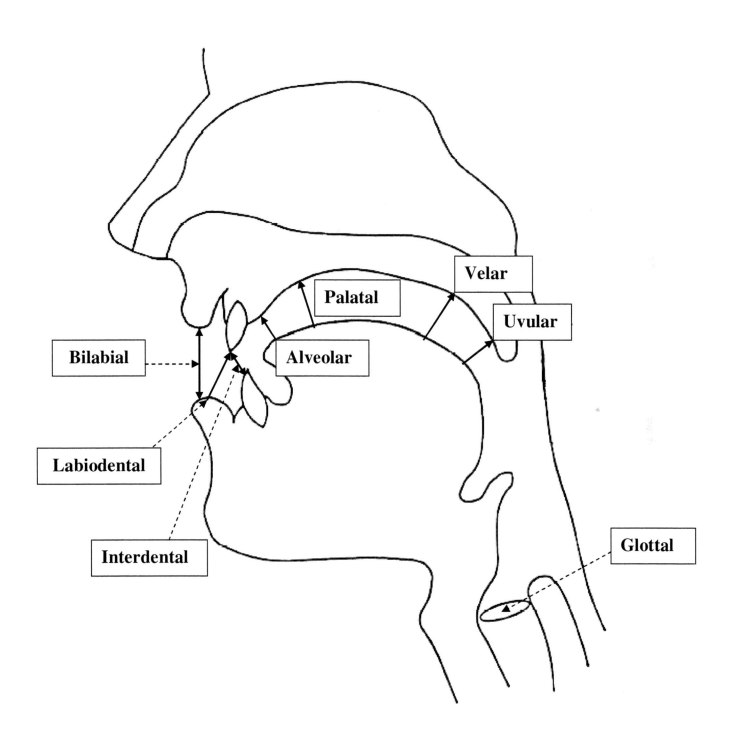

Bilabial

Labiodental

Interdental

Alveolar

Palatal

Velar

Uvular

Glottal

The Consonants of Standard American English (SAE)

It is important to think of three basic aspects[4] when describing consonants and to develop the habit of asking the following sets of questions in this order:

I. Is the consonant **voiced** or **voiceless**? That is, are the vocal cords activated or not in the production of this sound? And, when you think of this, remember to apply this only to the sound itself in isolation, not to the name of the letter in the English alphabet.

II. Where is the action taking place in the mouth (places of articulation)? Here we see the terms: **bilabials** [p, b, m, w, ʍ]; **labiodentals** [f, v]; **interdentals** [θ, ð]; **alveolars** [t, d, n, s, z, l, r]; **palatals** [š, ž, č, j, y]; **velars** [k, g, ŋ] and **glottals** [h, ʔ].

> **Places of Articulation**
> **Bilabials:** The action takes place between the two lips.
> **Labiodentals:** Between the lower lip and the upper teeth
> **Interdentals:** The tip of the tongue is between the teeth.
> **Alveolars:** The tip of the tongue is interacting with the ridge just behind the top front teeth.
> **Palatals:** The front half of the tongue is interacting in a generalized manner with the roof of the mouth from the alveolar ridge back to about the middle of the roof of the mouth (the hard palate).
> **Velars:** The upper back part of the tongue is interacting with the velum (the soft palate).
> **Glottals:** Action taking place right at the glottis or the vocal cords.

> **Manners of Articulation**
> **Stops:** These sounds are made by the release of a complete closure of the mouth.
> **Fricatives:** These are almost closures but not quite. They are so close to closure that they create turbulence. They get their names from this turbulence or the friction created.
> **Affricates:** You "start with a stop and release to a fricative." These are, in fact, consonant clusters although we do not perceive them that way.
> **Liquids:** Made with very little restriction of the air flow
> **Glides:** Made with even less restriction

III. How is the action being made (manners of articulation)? Here we see the terms: **stops** [p, b, m, t, d, n, k, g, ŋ, ʔ]; **fricatives** [f, v, θ, ð, s, z, š, ž, h]; **affricates** [č, j]; **liquids** [l, r] and **glides** [y, w].

---

[4] Please note that the terms presented here apply only to English.

All three of these criteria for the consonants of English can be summarized in the following chart:

	Bilabial	Labiodental	Interdental	Alveolar	Palatal	Velar	Glottal
Stop (oral) Voiced Voiceless	b p			d t		g k	?[5]
Stop(nasal) Voiced	m			n		ŋ	
Fricative Voiced Voiceless		v f	ð θ	z s	ž š		h
Affricate Voiced Voiceless					ǰ č		
Glide Voiced Voiceless	w ʍ[6]				y		
Liquid Voiced				l r			

Each of the consonants can be described in two ways:
  A. The official names as shown in the chart above
  B. The description of how you actually make the sound. This is far more helpful for you as educators. If you can accurately describe in physical terms how all of the sounds of English are made, you can go a long way toward solving hundreds of pronunciation problems for all levels of English instruction.

Steps in Making the Consonants:

b (voiced bilabial stop):
  1. Activate your vocal cords (what this means is that you must be prepared to vibrate the vocal cords just at the time of the release of this stop).
  2. Completely close your mouth between your lips.
  3. Build up a moderate amount of pressure within your mouth (this can actually be measured by PSI, pounds per square inch, exactly like the pressure in the tires of your car).

---

[5] The glottal stop is not considered a phoneme in English; so, it is not counted among the 25 consonants. Though it fits all the criteria for consonants, it is "heard" by English speakers simply as an allophone of /t/, or it is completely ignored as with vowel-beginning words such as *apple,* said in isolation or at the beginning of a sentence.

[6] This [ʍ] begins with a voiceless sound and turns into a voiced sound.

4. Release the pressure without producing any clear vowel afterwards. Just say [b-b-b]. Train yourself not to say the name of this letter in the English alphabet. The last part of the name consists of a vowel [i], and this only confuses the production of the consonant by itself.

č (voiceless palatal affricate, as in *church*):

1. Deactivate your vocal cords.
2. Make a [t]: a) completely close your mouth by placing the tip of your tongue on the alveolar ridge (you may tell students that this is just behind the upper teeth); b) build up pressure in your mouth; and c) release to the making of a [š].
3. Make a [š] by moving your tongue back from the alveolar ridge and by pressing upwards toward the palatal area, while continuing the flow of air with your vocal cords deactivated.
4. During the release the complete stop of the [t] is converted to a tight pressuring of your tongue against the palatal area. This is the fricative [š], but the whole sound, from start to finish, is perceived by English speakers as one sound; that is, one phoneme.

d (voiced alveolar stop):

1. Activate your vocal cords in preparation for the sound.
2. Completely close your mouth by placing the tip of your tongue on the alveolar ridge.
3. Build up pressure in your mouth.
4. Release to a nondescript sound, not a clear vowel as would be included in sounding out the name for this letter in English.

f (voiceless labiodental fricative):

1. Deactivate your vocal cords.
2. Place your lower lip tightly against your upper teeth. It is impossible to completely close this off because air can escape between your teeth. This escaping air between the teeth is what makes the turbulent sound of this fricative.
3. Blowing air out in this configuration will create the sound.

g (voiced velar stop):

1. Activate your vocal cords.

2. Press the back part of the main body of the tongue against the velum (soft palate) completely so that air cannot get through.
3. Build up pressure.
4. Release to a nondescript sound.

h (voiceless glottal fricative):
1. Deactivate your vocal cords.
2. Produce moderate constriction right at the vocal cords themselves.
3. Release air through this constriction.

j (voiced palatal affricate):
1. Activate your vocal cords.
2. Make a [d]: a) completely close your mouth by placing the tip of your tongue on the alveolar ridge, b) build up pressure in your mouth, and c) release to the making of a [ž].
3. Make a [ž] by moving your tongue back from the alveolar ridge to the palatal area, releasing while continuing to activate your vocal cords.
4. During the release the complete stop of the [d] is converted to a tight pressuring of your tongue against the palatal area. This is the fricative [ž], but the whole sound, from start to finish, is perceived by English speakers as one sound; that is, one phoneme.

k (voiceless velar stop):
1. Deactivate your vocal cords.
2. Press the back part of the main body of your tongue against the velum completely so that air cannot get through.
3. Build up pressure.
4. Release to a nondescript sound.

l (voiced alveolar lateral liquid):
1. Activate your vocal cords.
2. Press the tip of your tongue firmly against your alveolar ridge.
3. Draw in both sides of your tongue so that air can escape along each side.
4. Let the voiced air escape in this way.

m (voiced bilabial nasal stop):
1. Activate your vocal cords.
2. Completely close your mouth between your lips while you open the nasal passage at the back of your throat.

3. Let the air escape in this way.

n (voiced alveolar nasal stop):
  1. Activate your vocal cords.
  2. Completely close your mouth by placing the tip of your tongue on the alveolar ridge while you open the nasal passage at the back of your throat.
  3. Let the air escape in this way.

ŋ (voiced velar nasal stop, as in *ring*):
  1. Activate your vocal cords.
  2. Completely close your mouth by placing the upper back of your tongue against the velum in the same place where you make a [k] or a [g].
  3. Let the air escape in this way.

p (voiceless bilabial stop):
  1. Deactivate your vocal cords.
  2. Completely close your mouth between your lips.
  3. Build up pressure in your mouth.
  4. Release to a nondescript sound (this should sound like whispering).

r (voiced alveolar liquid):[7]
  1. Activate your vocal cords.
  2. Raise the tip of your tongue up into a retroflex (curled back) position just behind the alveolar ridge without touching any part of the roof of your mouth.
  3. Let the voiced air escape in this way.

s (voiceless alveolar fricative):
  1. Deactivate your vocal cords.
  2. Push the tip of your tongue up very close to the alveolar ridge without actually touching it.
  3. Release air through this tight squeeze.

š (voiceless palatal fricative, as in *short*):
  1. Deactivate your vocal cords.

---

[7] Notice that this is almost the same name as that for the [l]. It is no small wonder that these two sounds create confusion in the minds of many ELs.

2. Press the front half of your tongue up very close to a generalized area of your hard palate.
3. Release air through this tight squeeze.

t (voiceless alveolar stop):
1. Deactivate your vocal cords.
2. Completely close your mouth by placing the tip of your tongue on the alveolar ridge.
3. Build up pressure in your mouth.
4. Release to a nondescript sound, not a clear vowel as would be included in the name for this letter in English.

θ (voiceless interdental fricative, as in *thin*):[8]
1. Deactivate your vocal cords.
2. Place the tip of your tongue directly between your teeth with more pressure exerted toward the upper teeth.
3. Release air in this way.

ð (voiced interdental fricative, as in *that*):
1. Activate your vocal cords.
2. Place the tip of your tongue directly between your teeth with more pressure exerted toward the upper teeth.
3. Release air in this way.

v (voiced labiodental fricative):
1. Activate your vocal cords.
2. Place your lower lip tightly against your upper teeth. It is impossible to completely close this off because air can escape between your teeth. This escaping air between your teeth is what makes the turbulent sound of this fricative.
3. Blowing air out in this configuration will create the sound.

---

[8] This sound and its voiced equivalent [ð] are two of the most challenging English sounds for speakers of many other languages. If you can help students to see that the issue is purely physical and if you can accurately describe to them how to make them, then you will have crossed one of the big hurdles in teaching pronunciation especially to adults. Because both of them occur right in the front of the mouth, bring small mirrors to each student and have them practice just watching themselves be able to produce the sound with really very little effort. There is no "mystery" to these sounds at all.

W (voiced bilabial glide):
1. Activate your vocal cords.
2. Draw your lips close to each other.
3. Release air in this way as you relax your lips.

M (voiceless bilabial glide, as in the older pronunciation of *what*):[9]
1. First deactivate your vocal cords and make an [h] by: a) producing moderate constriction right at the vocal cords themselves and b) releasing voiceless air through this constriction.
2. Now activate your vocal cords and release the first sound into a voiced bilabial glide [w] as described above.

y (voiced palatal glide):
1. Activate your vocal cords.
2. Push the front half of your tongue up toward the palatal area in a generalized way, but don't close it off.
3. Pull your tongue down from this area as you open your mouth to release the voiced air.

Z (voiced alveolar fricative):
1. Activate your vocal cords.
2. Push the tip of your tongue up very close to the alveolar ridge without actually touching it.
3. Release the voiced air through this tight squeeze.

Ž (voiced palatal fricative, as in *azure*):
1. Activate your vocal cords.
2. Press the front half of your tongue up very close to a generalized area of your hard palate.
3. Release the voiced air through this tight squeeze.

---

[9] This name is really only half of the story for this consonant. It actually begins as a voiceless glottal fricative [h] which releases to a voiced bilabial glide [w], a consonant cluster of sorts. This is the phoneme that is disappearing from American English.

124

The following list gives the phonetic symbols for the 25 consonant phonemes of Standard American English (SAE) along with examples of the range of English spellings that represent those phonemes:

The 25 Consonants of Standard American English In Simplified Phonetic Forms[10]
(Plus one "Odd Man Out:" The Glottal Stop [ʔ])

Phonetic Symbol:	Examples (initially, medially and finally [when possible]):
b	boot, trouble, barb
č	church, kitchen, situation, batch
d	dog, middle, ford
f	fog, phoneme, waffle, graph, laugh, half, huff
g	go, gurgle, blog, Salzburg
h	hot, half, who, rehabilitate, rehearse
j	jury, judge, gerrymander, budget, wedge
k	cat, kitchen, quicken, flick, Bolshevik, triptych, technique
l	leap, lord, Hillel, pillory, hall, tall
m	map, more, smile, commit, ham, comb
n	now, know, gnostic, snooze, window, minnow, grin
ŋ	singer, linger, sink, ring
p	pie, pay, pray, play, apple, simple, wimp, trip
r	rye, roar, ramble, gory, Laurie, hear, fire
s	so, sleeve, stretch, psyche, receive, listen, hats, miss
š	shine, sheer, washer, ration, fission, facial, wish
t	Tom, tease, Ptolemy, winter, attend, hunt, wished
θ	thatch, throw, thrive, ether, breath, wreath
ð	though, them, leather, heather, breathe, lathe
v	vole, vibrant, vixen, hover, shovel, grave, dove
w	way, waiver, quiet, swindle, our, cower
ʍ (hw)	why, whether, when (for a dwindling number of speakers)
y	yet, yesterday, university, cute, lawyer
z	zebra, xylophone, dizzy, business, logs, haze
ž	Jacque, azure, leisure, barrage, garage
ʔ	umbrella, aisle (the very first sound of these two when said in isolation), button, gluten, won't, don't (when these last two are followed by other words)

---

[10] Notice that these symbols appear to be the same as the symbols for the phonemes. Bear in mind, however, that /t/ is a much larger concept than [t]. [t] is a simplified version of the phonetic result produced by the mouth while /t/ incorporates all of the possible allophones for this phoneme. [t] is a real sound while /t/ is an abstract concept.

The Vowels of
Standard American English

Since all vowels are voiced and are made with no restriction of the airflow through the mouth, they are described by the position of the central bulge of the tongue within the oral cavity by the following three criteria:

1. Height of the tongue: high to mid-range to low
2. Front to back location of the tongue: front to central to back
3. Rounding or unrounding of the lips

The diagram below follows the general position and movement of the central bulge of the tongue as it forms the sound chamber in the mouth:

The 12 "Pure" Vowels and "Lesser Diphthongs"[11]

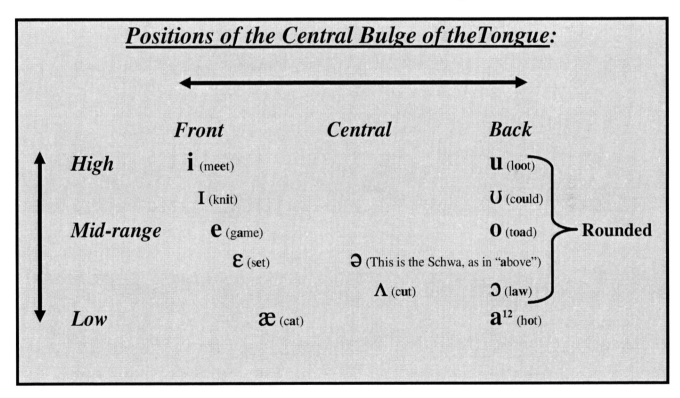

Positions of the Central Bulge of theTongue:

	Front	Central	Back	
High	i (meet)		u (loot)	
	I (knit)		U (could)	
Mid-range	e (game)		O (toad)	Rounded
	ɛ (set)	ə (This is the Schwa, as in "above")		
		Λ (cut)	ɔ (law)	
Low		æ (cat)	a[12] (hot)	

---

[11] See if you can identify which vowels in this chart are relatively pure and which ones are smaller versions of the three prominent diphthongs shown in the next chart.

[12] This symbol is a simplification for the actual vowel sound. Phoneticians will require ɑ for this back vowel and **a** for a more central and slightly higher vowel. However, the handwriting for these two symbols will create confusion for teachers. So, I have chosen one symbol for both. Also, notice that this is the only back vowel that is not rounded (rounding refers to the shape of the lips while making a vowel).

The 3 Prominent Diphthongs

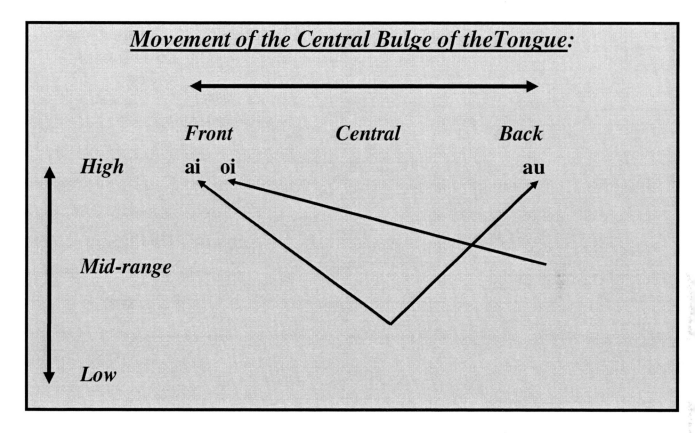

To produce all of these fifteen vowels, do the following:

1. Always activate your vocal cords for all of the vowels.

2. For the "pure" unrounded vowels (**i, ɪ, ɛ, æ, ə, ʌ** and **a**), position the central bulge of your tongue as described in the chart and do not round your lips. As you move from **i** to **a**, naturally your mouth will have to drop open more to accommodate the change in the tongue position.

3. For all of the rounded vowels (**u, ʊ, o** and **ɔ**) naturally you must round your lips.

4. For the "lesser diphthongs" (**e, ʊ** and **o**) your tongue must move during the vowel sound from the main sound to a slightly pronounced second sound. For example, to make an **e,** you finish this mid-range front vowel with a slight **i** sound. To make an **ʊ,** you finish this sound with a slight Schwa (**ə**). To make an **o,** you finish this sound with a slight **u.**

5. To make the prominent diphthongs you simply follow the tongue positions shown by the combined letters, following the movement of the arrows in the chart above.

6. The completion of all of these vowels occurs by the continuous outflow of voiced air from the mouth.

The following list gives the phonetic symbols for the 15 vowel phonemes of SAE along with examples of the range of English spellings that represent those phonemes:

The 15 Vowels of Standard American English In Simplified Phonetic Forms

Phonetic Symbol:	Examples (initially, medially and finally [when possible]):
a	arm, artist, artisan, honest, father, large, mama, papa, hurrah
æ	average, action, laugh, gadfly
ai	iron, aisle, icon, slice, height, choir, fly, high
au	out, hour, Howard, flour, how, now
e	aim, eight, aviary, game, bait, they, play
ɛ	every, expert, get, dead, said, quest
ə	above, apply, general, radium, sofa, America
i	eaten, elect, eel, reel, steal, people, deceive, flee, agree
ɪ	invite, interior, grin, slim, individual
o	over, aubergine, float, wrote, flow, so, though
ɔ	awe, autumn, awful, log, fall, fraught, law
oi	oil, ointment, foil, spoil, coy, ploy
u	ooze, rude, coot, newt, do, grew, flu, blue, through
ʊ	cookie, put, book, hood, should, butcher
ʌ	ugly, oven, glove, cut, does, gruff, hover

This chapter provides the basis for understanding what speakers of SAE actually do to make the sounds of the phonemes. Your ability to teach pronunciation will be greatly enhanced if you use the knowledge of this chapter to limit your instruction to the actual physical process that takes place in the vocal tract.

There is no mystery to it. If students get stuck in trying to produce a particular sound of SAE, most probably they are working on a process that is unrelated to the actual production of the sound. Bring small, individual mirrors into the classroom so that they can see exactly what they are doing. You, the instructor, are now able to tell them exactly what to do. Unless there is some physical impairment, all of them will be able to produce these sounds precisely as Americans do, and this will especially help adult ELs as they learn how to function in this society. It can raise their self-esteem dramatically as they struggle to speak fluently.

Test Your Knowledge (Exercise 18)
"Using the IPA"

Now that you have some familiarity with the International Phonetic Alphabet, try your hand at writing in it. Put the following two sentences in the IPA:

A. Somebody please tell me why linguistics is considered so boring.

[

]

B. I just can't get enough of phonemes.

[

]

C. **č** is a voiceless palatal affricate.

[

]

Test Your Knowledge (Exercise 19)
"Making the true sounds of difficult English phonemes"
<u>Consonants</u>

[r] and [θ] are two of the hardest consonants for ELs to make in American English. Borrow from the explanation in the book, but, most importantly, use your own words to describe how to make these two. Remember to go over the three principal aspects of each consonant and to come back to the one of these three that is giving problems to your ELs (1. Voiced/voiceless sound, 2. Where it is being made in the mouth, and 3. How you make this sound at that location in the mouth):

[r]

[θ] (as in <u>thin</u>)

130

Test Your Knowledge (Exercise 20)
"Making the true sounds of difficult English phonemes"
<u>Vowels</u>

The rules are different for vowels. There is no such thing as a voiceless vowel. By their nature they have to be voiced. The sounds of vowels come through the mouth unrestricted, and the difference between them is the result of 3 things: 1. The position of the central bulge of the tongue: high or low, 2. Whether the central bulge of the tongue is toward the front or toward the back in the mouth, and 3. Whether the lips are rounded or not. Describe the making of [ɔ] as in the vowel sound of *law, caught, ball:*

A. High or low in the mouth?

B. Front or back in the mouth?

C. Rounded or unrounded lips?

Congratulations! You Made It!

You came through the minefield, and you are still in one piece.

You have visited all of Nim Chimpsky's villages, and hopefully you have had some good laughs and a good cup of coffee (or perhaps a glass of wine) in each village as you acquired these fundamental concepts of linguistics. These enjoyable aspects are the essential involvement of the right brain along with the work of the left brain's linear, more analytic approach to all of this. What have you learned in each of these villages, and specifically which of these concepts and skills will you take into your own classrooms?

The purpose of this book is to assist you in becoming airborne with English so that you can be a powerful catalyst for your own students to become airborne and in command of this amazing language. It is our hope that from now on you will incorporate the following new approaches toward English for yourself and for your students:

1. Bring your unconscious knowledge of English to the surface.

2. Objectify the vast ocean of knowledge you already have of English and name its crucial aspects.

3. Consistently apply these new skills to your own classrooms.

4. Have fun in the process.

All the best in your teaching!

*Books you can't live without if you are teaching adults

References

American Heritage Dictionary of the English Language, The.
> 2000 (4th edition) Boston: Houghton Mifflin. This is the best series of reference works for general use.

Ammer, C.
> 1997 *The American Heritage Dictionary of Idioms.*
> Boston: Houghton Mifflin.

Baker, M. C.
> 2001 *The Atoms of Language: The Mind's Hidden Rules of Grammar.* New York: Basic Books.

Cambridge University Press. Their catalogs for English Language learning provide excellent materials for both American and British English.

Celce-Murcia, M.
> 1999 (2nd edition) *Teaching English as a Second or Foreign Language.* Boston: Heinle & Heinle.

*Celce-Murcia, M., D. M. Brinton & J. M. Goodwin.
> 1996 *Teaching Pronunciation: A Reference for Teachers of English to Speakers of Other Languages.* Cambridge University Press.

*Celce-Murcia, M. & D. Larsen-Freeman.
> 1999 (2nd edition) *The Grammar Book: An ESL/EFL Teacher's Course.* Boston: Heinle & Heinle.

Chicago Manual of Style, The.
> 1993 (14th edition) Chicago: University of Chicago Press.

Chomsky, N.
> 1957 *Syntactic Structures.* The Hague: Mouton.
> 1965 *Aspects of the Theory of Syntax.* Cambridge, MA: MIT Press.
> 1972 (2nd edition) *Language and the Mind.* New York: Harcourt Brace Jovanovich.
> 2000 *The Architecture of Language.* Oxford University Press.

Chomsky, N. & M. Halle.
> 1968 *The Sound Pattern of English.* New York: Harper & Row.

*Collins COBUILD Advanced Dictionary of American English.
> 2007 Boston: Thomson/Heinle.

134

Collins COBUILD Intermediate Dictionary of American English.
 2008 Boston: Thomson/Heinle.
Cook, G.
 2000 *Language Play, Language Learning.* Oxford University Press.
Coulmas, R.
 2003 *Writing Systems: An Introduction to their Linguistic Analysis.*
 Cambridge University Press.
Daniels, P. T. & W. Bright (eds).
 1996 *The World's Writing Systems.* New York: Oxford University
 Press.
Fillmore, L. W. and C. E. Snow. *What Teachers Need to Know about
Language.* Washington, DC: US Department of Education and the
Center for Applied Linguistics, 2000.
Firsten, R. & P. Killian.
 1994 *Troublesome English: A Teaching Grammar for ESOL
Instructors.* Englewood Cliffs, NJ: Prentice Hall Regents.
Flexner, S. B. & A. H. Soukhanov.
 1997 *Speaking Freely: A Guided Tour of American English.* Oxford
University Press.

*Flower, J.
 2005 *Phrasal Verb Organiser with Mini-Dictionary.* Boston:
Thomson/Heinle.
Fromkin, V., R. Rodman & N. Hyams.
 2003 (7th edition) *An Introduction to Language.* Boston:
Thomson/Heinle.
Heinle & Heinle (see Thomson/Heinle).

*Hopper, V. F. et al.
 2000 (5th edition) *Essentials of English: A Practical Handbook Covering
All the Rules of English Grammar and Writing Style.* New
York: Barron's Educational Series.
International Phonetic Association.
 1999 *Handbook of the International Phonetic Association.*
Cambridge University Press.
Iowa, University of. *Phonetics* (an A/V depiction of the sounds of English,
German and Spanish, the movement of the tongue within the
vocal tract for all of the phonemes of each language).
www.uiowa.edu/~acadtech/phonetics
IPA font for English: Download "Newbury SILDoulos" from
www.fonts4free.net/newbury-sildoulos-font.html

Katzner, K.
  1995 (2nd edition) *The Languages of the World*. London: Routledge & Kegan Paul.

Ladefoged, P.
  1996   *The Sounds of the World's Languages*. Oxford: Blackwell Publishers.

Lakoff, G.
  1987   *Women, Fire, and Dangerous Things: What Categories Reveal about the Mind*. Chicago: University of Chicago Press.
  2004   *Don't Think of an Elephant! Know Your Values and Frame the Debate*. White River Junction, VT: Chelsea Green Publishing Company.

Lakoff, G., & M. Johnson.
  1980   *Metaphors We Live By*. Chicago: Chicago University Press.

Lakoff, R.
  1990   *Talking Power: The Politics of Language*. New York: Basic Books.

Langacker, R. W.
  1968   *Language and Its Stucture: Some Fundmental Linguistic Concepts*.   New York: Harcourt, Brace & World.

Lewis, G. L.
  1967   *Turkish Grammar*. Oxford: Clarendon Press.

Lyovin, A. V.
  1997   *An Introduction to Languages of the World*. New York: Oxford University Press.

Makkai, A., M. T. Boatner & J. E. Gates.
  1995   *A Dictionary of American Idioms*. New York: Barron's Educational Series.

Matthews, P. J.
  1997   *The Concise Oxford Dictionary of Linguistics*. Oxford University Press

McCrum, R., W. Cran & R. MacNeil.
  1986   *The Story of English*. New York: Viking.

McWhorter, J.
  2001   *The Power of Babel: A Natural History of Language*. New York: Times Books.

Morenberg, M.
  2002 (3rd edition) *Doing Grammar*. Oxford University Press.

National Institute for Literacy
  1992   *National Adult Literacy Survey*. www.nifl.gov

136

*_Newbury House Dictionary of American English: The Core of English Language Learning_
>2004 (4th edition). Boston: Thomson/Heinle.

Oxford Collocations Dictionary for Students of English.
>2002   Oxford University Press.

Oxford English Dictionary, The.
>(most recent edition) Oxford University Press.

Oxford University Press. Their catalogs for English Language learning provide excellent materials for both American and British English.

*Oxford, R. L.
>1990   _Language Learning Strategies: What Every Teacher Should Know_. Boston: Heinle & Heinle.

Pennycook, A.
>2001   _Critical Applied Linguistics: A Critical Introduction_. Mahwah, NJ: Lawrence Erlbaum Associates.

Pinker, S.
>1994   _The Language Instinct_. New York: William Morrow.
>1999   _Words and Rules: The Ingredients of Language_. New York: HarperCollins.
>2007   _The Stuff of Thought: Language as a Window into Human Nature_. New York: Viking Penguin.

Ruhlen, M.
>1994   _On the Origin of Languages_. Stanford University Press.

*Spears, R. A.
>2005   _McGraw-Hill's Dictionary of American Idioms and Phrasal Verbs_. New York: McGraw-Hill.

Statistical Abstract of the United States.
>1990   (110th edition).
>2002   (122nd edition). Washington, DC: U.S. Department of Commerce and the U.S. Census Bureau.

*Swan, M. & B. Smith (eds).
>2001   _Learner English: A Teacher's Guide to Interference and Other Problems_. Cambridge University Press, 2001 (2nd edition).

Tannen, D.
>1990   _You Just Don't Understand: Women and Men in Conversation_. New York: Ballantine.

✛Thomson/Heinle, the best publisher of ESL materials for General American English. Order a new catalog of these materials every year. This publisher used to be called Heinle & Heinle. 877-NEED-ESL (or) www.heinle.com

Thurman, S.
 2002 *The Everything Grammar and Style Book: All the Rules You Need to Know to Master Great Writing*. Avon, MA: Adams Media Corp.

Wills, G.
 1992 *Lincoln at Gettysburg: The Words That Remade America*. New York: Touchstone.

Winchester, S.
 1999 *The Professor and the Madman: A Tale of Murder, Insanity, and the Making of the Oxford English Dictionary*. New York: HarperPerennial.

*****Wright, J.**
 2002 *Idioms Organiser: Organised by Metaphor, Topic and Key Word*. Boston: Thomson/Heinle.

Index

To order:

1. Additional copies of this book, or
2. The answer key to the exercises in the book (ISBN #978-0-9778-0292-0),

Please visit the website for the
International Institute of Language and Culture:

www.linguisticsforeducators.com

The website describes the work of IILC and includes examples of outstanding papers and lesson plans created by former students of linguistics.

To communicate with us directly send an email to:

linguisticsforeducators@yahoo.com